FOUNDATIONS OF DISTANCE EDUCATION

ROUTLEDGE STUDIES IN DISTANCE EDUCATION
Series editor: Desmond Keegan

FOUNDATIONS OF DISTANCE EDUCATION

Third Edition

Desmond Keegan

London and New York

First published 1986 by Croom Helm
Second edition 1990 by Routledge
Reprinted 1991, 1994
Third edition 1996 by Routledge
11 New Fetter Lane, London EC4P 4EE

Simultaneously published in the USA and Canada
by Routledge
29 West 35th Street, New York, NY 10001

Typeset in Palatino by
J&L Composition Ltd, Filey, North Yorkshire
Printed and bound in Great Britain by
Biddles Ltd, Guildford and King's Lynn

British Library Cataloguing in Publication Data
A catalogue record for this book is available from the British Library

Library of Congress Cataloguing in Publication Data
Keegan, Desmond.
Foundations of distance education/Desmond Keegan. – 3rd ed.
p.   cm. – (Routledge studies in distance education)
Includes bibliographical references and index.
1. Distance education.   I. Title.   II. Series.
LC5800.K43   1996
378'.03–dc20   95–53943
CIP
ISBN 0–415–13909–0

For L.L.,
Desmond Jnr,
Martin and
Patricia

CONTENTS

CONTENTS

Part IV Evaluation

FIGURES

TABLES

PREFACE

Foundations of Distance Education was written to give a first introduction to distance education for readers who are new to the field and a first overview of the field for students, administrators and practitioners in distance systems. The book has also served as a text for university courses on distance education.

First published in 1986, a second edition was produced in 1990. Rapid developments in the 1990s have created the need for a third edition.

One of the strengths of the first and second editions was an in-depth analysis of the socialist distance education systems of Central and Eastern Europe. This has needed to be completely recast in the light of political changes at the start of the 1990s and the abandonment of the socialist distance education model which followed. A number of features of the model are pre-served in the world's largest system of the late 1990s, the *Dianda* network in China, and, where appropriate, illustrations are provided from that system.

It is pleasing to record that the field of distance education, still fragile when this book was first designed, is vibrant today. It has received great impetus from the revolution in electronic telecom-munications of the late 1980s. The challenge for the field in the twenty-first century will be the harnessing of the new telecom-munications technologies, already developed but not yet inte-grated into distance education theory and practice, ranging from fibre-to-the-local-loop videoconferencing to the desktop to mul-timedia in the home.

I express my sincere gratitude to Michel Moreau of Poitiers, Wei Runfang of Nanjing, Ian Small of Armidale and Joanne East of Gainesville, who generously contributed much of the material for Chapter 11, and to Michael G. Moore of Pennsylvania State University.

Desmond Keegan
Dublin
October 1995

ABBREVIATIONS

The following abbreviations are used from time to time especially in lists of references:

CCTVU   Central Chinese Television University
CMA   Computer-marked assignment
CNED   Centre National d'Enseignement à Distance (National Centre for Distance Education)
CU   Conventional university
DIFF   Deutsches Institut für Fernstudienforschung, Tübingen
DTU   Distance teaching university
FeU   Fernuniversität–Gesamthochschule, Hagen
ICDE   International Council for Distance Education
DETC   Distance Education and Training Council
OU   Open University
OUUK   Open University of the United Kingdom
TMA   Tutor-marked assignment
UNE   University of New England, Armidale, Australia
UNED   Universidad Nacional de Educación a Distancia
UNISA   University of South Africa, Pretoria
ZIFF   Zentrales Institut für Fernstudienforschung, Fernuniversität, Hagen.

Part I

THE CONCEPT OF DISTANCE EDUCATION

1

THE STUDY OF DISTANCE EDUCATION

> It is the development of distance education as an academic discipline that will have the most profound effect on its practice in the future.
>
> Eric Gough, 1984

CONTEXT

On the occasion of the 25th anniversary of the foundation of the Open University of the United Kingdom, its Vice-Chancellor wrote:

> In the summer of 1970 a first cohort of 25,000 students were admitted to a new university. They took a risk in joining the Open University. It was an untried institution whose radical innovations of open admission and multimedia distance learning had provoked hostility among politicians and scepticism in educational circles. Now, a generation later, we can see that these intrepid students actually pioneered the most important educational innovation of their time.
>
> (Daniel 1995: x)

The generation from 1970 to 2000 is witnessing a development of the whole field of distance education which paralleled the success and achievements of the Open University. There has been a remarkable change in the quality, the quantity, the status and the influence of distance education provision. This was linked to a world-wide shift from private to public provision. From 1870 to 1970 most of the systems were proprietary and the field was known as 'correspondence study' or 'home study' or

3

'external studies'. Hostility from the education establishment was rarely far from the surface. Today most governments in the world are providing or considering introducing distance education and are studying its role as a complement to conventional provision.

In the late 1990s distance education is a valued component of many education systems and has proved its worth in areas where traditional schools, colleges and universities have difficulties in meeting demand. A good example is very large systems.

Many countries of the world today need educational systems capable of competently handling very large student bodies totalling 100,000 or more students at a time. Governments in both developed and developing countries no longer have the money to build and maintain buildings for 100,000 students a year, or if they did they would not put the money into educational buildings because of changed political and developmental priorities (Coombs 1978). The answer must, therefore, come from distance education. There were in 1995 ten distance systems competently handling at least 100,000 students at a time (Table 1.1). All of these are national institutions of great prestige and excellent quality. None is new or experimental. Most have decades of experience and tens of thousands of graduates already integrated into the national workforce. Such institutions form an important focus for the study of distance education and underline the contribution of this form of education to developed and emerging economies alike.

Table 1.1 Very large distance systems

Country	Name of institution	Enrolment	Foundation
China	CCTVU network	852,000	1979
Turkey	Anadolu University	600,000	1982
France	CNED	350,000	1939
Indonesia	Universitas Terbuka	353,000	1984
Thailand	Sukothai Thamatirat OU	350,000	1978
India	Indira Ghandhi N OU	242,000	1985
Korea	National Open University	200,000	1972
United Kingdom	Open University	200,000	1969
Spain	UNED	140,000	1972
South Africa	UNISA	130,000	1949
Total		3,417,000	

Source: Institutional statistics 1995

In the years 1996 to 2000 distance education will play a new and crucial role as a complement to schools, colleges and universities in many national education systems. Illustrations from the United Kingdom, the United States, China, France and the European Union are cited briefly here.

In the United Kingdom there are distance programmes from the University of London and a range of conventional universities, especially former polytechnics, in addition to the Open University with its headquarters at Milton Keynes. At further education level many of the colleges of further education offer distance or flexible or open courses and there is a vigorous proprietary sector whose origins go back nearly 150 years. Total enrolment at any one time is unlikely to be less than 500,000, many of whom are studying for nationally recognized university degrees.

The student of distance education will find a complex array of provision in the United States in the late 1990s ranging from correspondence courses to advanced synchronous technologies. No fewer than 5 million are enrolled in proprietary correspondence courses at any one time, with courses from each branch of the armed forces, many government departments and many religious foundations (Moore 1995a). An additional 250,000 are enrolled in independent study courses from over seventy American universities. College-level television courses, known as telecourses; teleconferencing, provided either by two-way video or one-way video with two-way audio; audioconferencing; audiographics, cable and computer networking have all contributed to an explosion of interest in distance education in the United States. Satellite teleconferencing is used by many of America's big companies with 60,000 receive sites in 1995, and there is comprehensive K–12 provision for children, including the Star Schools project. Portway and Lane (1994) list at least eighty major state or federal distance education initiatives ranging from America Online to World Classroom International Telecommunications Network. Total annual enrolment is estimated at 8 million.

Distance education in China can be traced back to the provision of correspondence courses in the early 1900s. TV-based university-level programmes were started in the early 1960s, disbanded during the Cultural Revolution, and restarted in 1979. The present system, known as *Dianda*, is a network comprising a central open university in Beijing which develops courses and forty-three open universities in each province and major municipality (Wei and Tong 1994); 1995 enrolment is 852,000. To this must be added a correspondence system at university and sub-university level, and a self-study for university examination system, both dealing with 1 million students annually.

Massive government involvement in distance education at all levels is a characteristic of France. The invasion of France in 1939 led to the foundation of the Centre National d'Enseignement par Correspondance to provide correspondence courses for displaced schoolchildren. After the war an adult section was added. In 1995 enrolment had grown to 350,000 from 170 countries, making the Centre National d'Enseignement à Distance, as it is now called, Europe's largest public education institution. Awards are available at a distance at every level from primary, secondary, vocational, technical, teacher-training through to university level. There is no open university but a small provision of 35,000 from conventional universities with a further 250,000 enrolled annually in private institutions.

A recent study (Keegan 1994) of distance training in the European Union showed that almost 2.25 million were enrolled in the, then, twelve member states. Half were in government-organized distance training institutions; half in proprietary. On the assumption that each student paid an annual fee of ECU 500, the annually recurring market is quantified at over 1 billion ECU. This study took no account of in-house or corporate distance training provision. To this training provision must be added 366,212 enrolled in the European open universities and an estimated 130,000 in distance programmes from conventional universities in Europe.

FIELD OF STUDY

Glimpses have been given above of the international richness and complexity that confront the student of distance education in the late 1990s. Compared to the study of conventional education it remains a relatively small field of study with an estimated 30 million, mostly adults, enrolled in distance education programmes world-wide compared to 600 million, mainly children, enrolled in schools, colleges or universities. It is, none the less, a new, vibrant and rapidly developing field of study. A notable factor in its development has been the range of technologies for communication at a distance that have been developed in the last decade.

A major task is the analysis of the breathtaking array of technologies already developed by the telecommunications industry and now ready for implementation in distance education. These include: universal mobile telephony, satellite virtual classrooms, universal personal telephony, fibre-to-the-local-loop, two-way video codec systems, videoconferencing to the desktop, broadband ISDN, the Internet, and multimedia to the home. The didactic possibilities of these technologies are immense and although they will have implications for students who travel to schools, colleges or universities, their major application will be for those who cannot attend classes or choose to study at a distance.

Recent attempts in the literature (Garrison 1985, Nipper 1989, Bates 1995) to analyse the development of the use of technology in distance education into three 'generations' are not followed here. The perspective is, rather, the contribution of distance education to educational provision.

If one attempted to analyse educational provision from the point of view of distance education one might identify three differing structures: conventional provision; teaching at a distance; teaching face-to-face at a distance. Each of these complements the others and enriches the possibilities of offering education to learners.

Conventional education

Conventional provision is the normal offering of education in schools, colleges and universities today. Its characteristic structures are the dialogue, the lecture developed by the medieval universities, the tutorial and seminar added by the humanists and, more recently, the laboratory practical, the field trip and periods of study in the library or resource centre. Its characteristic technologies today are the overhead projector and the white (or black) board, technologies which require the students to travel to the institution for the purposes of learning.

Teaching at a distance

The history of teaching at a distance begins 150 years ago. Distance education was not possible without the developments of technology, especially in transportation and communication, associated with the Industrial Revolution. Teaching at a distance is characterized by the separation of teacher and learner and of the learner from the learning group, with the interpersonal face-to-face communication of conventional education being replaced by an apersonal mode of communication mediated by technology. This form of education is provided today by correspondence schools, open universities and distance or external departments of conventional colleges and universities.

Teaching face to face at a distance

The possibility of teaching face to face at a distance was achieved by an electronics revolution in the 1980s. The deregulation of the telecommunications industry allied to the speeding up of chips and the introduction of broadband technologies brought about this veritable revolution. The German scholar, Peters (1991) had argued that there was something unsettling about a form of education (distance education) in which interpersonal communication and face-to-face interaction in the learning group were eliminated, as these were regarded as cultural imperatives for education in East and West. Now these characteristics can be electronically recreated.

Virtual or electronic classrooms can now be linked by satellite or by compressed video codec technology or by full bandwith links, making it possible for the first time in history to teach face to face at a distance. The lecturer can see and hear the students present in the class and also all the other students at the other sites hundreds or thousands of kilometres away. All the students at all the locations can see and hear the lecturer and all other students in the system. The interaction of face-to-face education has been recreated electronically.

As the twenty-first century approaches, conventional face-to-face teaching in schools, colleges and universities continues to prosper but it is complemented by correspondence, audio, video and computer technologies from correspondence schools and open universities throughout the world. Both are enriched by the availability of virtual systems in which the face-to-face interpersonal communication of conventional education can be achieved at a distance.

The focus of this book is distance education, systems based on teaching at a distance. Conventional systems are considered the work of other scholars. Virtual systems based on (electronically) teaching face to face at a distance is considered a new and cognate field of study which already has important realizations like the foundation of the Open University of Catalonia in Barcelona in 1994 as a virtual university rather than an open university and a developing literature like Portway and Lane's *Guide to Teleconferencing and Distance Learning* (1994). The theoretical analyses of virtual education, however, have not yet been addressed by the literature: is it a subset of distance education or to be regarded as a separate field of educational endeavour? What are its didactic structures? What is the relationship of its cost effectiveness and of its educational effectiveness to distance education and to conventional education? All that can be attempted here is a presentation of the differing characteristics of distance education and virtual education and a listing of the advantages and the disadvantages of virtual systems.

The differences between distance education and virtual education are perceived as:

- *time synchronous technology*: distance education uses mainly time asynchronous technologies; virtual education uses mainly time synchronous technologies;
- *access*: the goal of distance education as enunciated by Wedemeyer (1981) is to provide courses any time, any place, anywhere there are students or only one student; virtual education reimposes much of the constraints of conventional education by requiring students to travel to virtual classrooms at fixed times on fixed days to join a learning group;
- *economics*: the basis of distance education economics (Chapter 10) is that institutions do not have to build and maintain buildings for distance students and that economies of scale can be achieved that are not available to conventional systems; virtual education reimposes much of the economic constraints of conventional systems;
- *didactics*: the didactic skills required in the electronic classroom reintroduce many of the skills of the school class or university lecture in contrast to the development of learning materials and the skills of teaching from them, often many years later, that is characteristic of distance education;

- *market*: the distance education market is, in the main, based on the availablity of educational qualifications by time asynchronous technologies; it has yet to be demonstrated worldwide that there is a market for students travelling to electronic classrooms for synchronous transmissions at scheduled times.

It is acknowledged that in a few years time the videoconferencing window now available on some personal computers will become standard on the motherboard and the experience of compressed video face-to-face synchronous communication will become generally available.

It is too early to suggest whether virtual systems will in the future be studied as a subset of distance education research or of conventional education research or as a field of study in its own right. This book considers the study of virtual and electronic classrooms as an important and complex field, still in its beginnings, with a unique contribution to make to educational knowledge and will refer to virtual systems where appropriate.

AIMS

This book attempts to respond to the call made over two decades ago by Moore, then of the University of Wisconsin at Madison and today at Pennsylvania State University:

> As we continue to develop various non-traditional methods of reaching the growing numbers of people who cannot, or who will not, attend conventional institutions but who choose to learn apart from their teachers, we should direct some of our resources to the macrofactors:
>
> - describing and defining the field
> - discriminating between the various components of this field
> - identifying the critical elements of the various forms of teaching and learning
> - building a theoretical framework which will embrace this whole area of education.
>
> (Moore 1973: 661)

Moore's call went largely unheeded. A theoretical framework to embrace this whole area of education has yet to be erected.

This is grave because distance education purports to make available a parallel provision of education to that of conventional schools, colleges, and universities. Unlike other methods of teaching or modes of operation with which they are sometimes bracketed, distance systems claim to provide a complete educational coverage, equal in quality and status to that of conventional provision, encompassing every stage of the educational process from application, enrolment, and counselling through to examination and certification many years later.

Most research in this field has been practical rather than theoretical. While research on the practice of distance education is important and fundamental it is incidental and peripheral to a firmly based theory of distance education. A theory is something that eventually can be reduced to a phrase, a sentence or a paragraph and which, while subsuming all the practical research, gives the foundation on which structures of need, purpose, and administration can be erected. A firmly based theory of distance education will be one which can provide the touchstone against which decisions – political, financial, educational, and social – can be taken with confidence. Such a theoretical basis would replace the *ad hoc* way of responding to 'crisis' situations which have frequently characterized this field of education.

Twenty-two years later Moore returned to the theme. As a result of a conference at the American Center for the Study of Distance Education he listed his agenda for distance education research. Among the topics are:

- The legitimacy of distance education in the professional lives of faculty and administrators and the attendant change processes necessary to provide distance education with 'value added' for these professionals.
- Finance and financial models. Illustrative questions include 'What is the efficiency of investment in distance education programs? and 'How is it measured'.
- Access, equity and the social impact of programs, especially as the 'information highway' increasingly encourages a market-driven concept of distance education. What is the socio-economic impact of such programs, and what consumer protection policies may be called for?

- Applying the results of research. What change models help determine how to successfully apply the information being revealed by research? What are the benefits, and what are the penalties, of applying this information?
(Moore 1995b: 2)

Although written from a United States conventional university perspective, this is a useful listing of the concerns for the foundations of distance education as the twentieth century comes to its end.

PREMISES

In attempting to provide a guide to theory and practice in distance education the following assumptions are made:

- Distance education is a coherent and distinct field of educational endeavour: it embraces programmes at a distance at primary and secondary, technical and further, college and university levels in both public and private sectors. It has existed for over a hundred years and is to be found today in most countries.
- Distance education is a system of education. It can provide a complete educational programme for both children and adults outside of, and distinct from, conventional, oral, group-based provision. It has its own laws of didactical structure and its own quasi-industrial administrative procedures.
- Distance education is a form of education fraught with problems for administrators, teachers, and students. It is characterized by the fragility of the non-traditional in education. These difficulties concern the quality, quantity, and status of education at a distance. Good practice in distance education seeks to provide solutions for these inherent difficulties.
- Distance education is a needed component of most national education systems.

This study does not seek to promote distance education. Rather it seeks to analyse it from as neutral a standpoint as possible and present it with both its strengths and weaknesses underlined. In doing this an attempt is made not to limit the research to the English-speaking tradition in education because the contribution of the English-speaking countries is only a part of a much more complex whole. Thus much of the basic distance education research in the period 1960–70 was done in German; the basic institutional model is probably French; in recent years much progress has been reported from Spanish-speaking countries; and this book is a much altered version of a series of lectures first delivered in Italian.

EDUCATIONAL RESEARCH

Where does the study of distance education lie within the discipline of education? Many universities have a faculty for teaching and research in the discipline of education. Most faculties of education are subdivided into departments or fields of teaching and research. Most faculties of education carry on research and teach in a selection of fields depending on student need, staff expertise, or government direction. Some of the fields (philosophy of education, educational psychology) are often regarded as essential. Some (special education) are in vogue today; some (comparative education) are in decline. Some (adult education, distance education, educational administration, educational technology) are more specialized and departments dealing with these fields may not be found in many universities.

This book regards distance education as a distinct field of educational research and teaching within the discipline of education. It is considered to have links to other fields within the discipline of education, notably educational technology, adult education, and the study of non-traditional/open systems.

HISTORY OF DISTANCE EDUCATION RESEARCH

Academic research in distance education reached a level of maturity compatible with the emergence of a new field within education by the early 1970s. Although noteworthy contributions had already been made by individual researchers, amongst whom one would certainly include Childs (1963) from the University of Lincoln at Nebraska, Wedemeyer (1963) from the University of Wisconsin at Madison and Holmberg (1960) from Malmö in Sweden, a major development came from a group of researchers whom one might call 'The Tübingen Group'.

The Tübingen Group comprised, amongst others, Dohmen

(1967), Graff (1964), Peters (1965), Delling (1966) and Rebel (1971). To this group can be attributed the identification of what Sparkes (1983: 180) calls 'the emergence of a new set of problems which is essential for an academic discipline'. By the early 1970s the Tübingen Group had published at least sixty research studies in a number of series which laid the foundations for the new field of educational research. Dohmen and Peters had defined and established the extent of the field, Delling had determined its history, and Peters had identified its particular focus which distinguished it from all other fields of educational research.

THE MID–1970S TO TODAY

The Tübingen group dispersed in the mid-1970s. Dohmen returned to the University of Tübingen, Peters and Graff transferred to the Fernuniversität, Delling and Rebel remained at the German Institute for Distance Education (DIFF). Few researchers in the English-speaking world built on the foundations laid by the Tübingen Group, though their work is cited by Holmberg, Bååth, and Wedemeyer.

The early 1970s saw the creation of a series of distance institutions for which 'newness' was politically important. These institutions seemed slow to align themselves with an established field, in existence for 100 years, found in every country of the world and for which the central focus was the abandonment of what had been a cultural imperative for university education since its inception: face-to-face interpersonal communication in the learning group. Researchers at these new open universities tended to align themselves with established fields of research that had a similarity to distance education but which would vigorously defend the role of interpersonal face-to-face communication in education (adult education, educational technology).

By the late 1970s terminology was clarified and progress was made towards definition (see Chapter 3). The 1980s saw an exponential growth in the literature on distance education, the foundation of a number of academic journals, and the development of research in sub-fields like course design, economics of distance education, student support services, and media in distance education. With the mid-1980s came the first courses for university credit in distance education.

METHODOLOGY

Considerable thought in preparing this study has been given to evolving a methodology for presenting the reader with a guide to this field of educational activity. A methodology was needed that would lead to knowledge and understanding. It had to be capable of describing and defining the field of distance education; it had to discriminate between the institutional types, the didactic strategies, the varying media that constitute this field; it had to be able to identify both those forms of teaching and learning which are seen as constituents of distance education and those that lie outside it.

In order to be successful as a guide, the methodology chosen had to be able to take account of the context and complexity of the field and to get to the real phenomenon of distance education and not some 'scientific' abstraction. It had to cover 100 years of history and the world-wide activity of the present time.

As well as charting the fragile theoretical underpinnings that scholars have supplied to date, the aim was to provide a guide to help administrators make sensible decisions and to help practitioners choose good models. Scientific research is ill at ease in the context of a guide. The controlled experiment, which is the linchpin of science's insistence on the reproducibility of data, involves ensuring that the normal variability of the environment is kept within specified limits. It is exactly the variability of the environment that a good guide should reflect. Further, the nature of scientific research, in which one attempts to analyse educational problems in terms of distinct causal theories, is out of place in an area where management rather than pedagogy is the key problem encountered. When the management of quasi-industrial processes is central to an educational system what is needed is not normative scientific study of special approaches to pedagogy but problem-based case-studies that can provide guides to good practice. Happily, narrow scientific research is not the only way to knowledge and understanding. Other methods can lead to valid explanations of the complex world of distance education systems.

PROCEDURE

The methodology adopted attempts to be synergistic; that is, it attempts to find a way to cope with the complexity of the educational environment and the inter-connectedness of human and institutional relationships. Another element that synergistic theories and methodologies seek to encapsulate is experience. Experience is of particular importance in this study: we are concerned here with the experience of the dedicated distance education tutor, the experience and common sense of the practised administrator, and it is important that such experience should not be eliminated by the methodology chosen.

In its actual execution, the study developed in four stages with extensive feedback mechanisms linking the various periods of research.

Stage 1

A Delphi-like approach was first used for a review of the literature. In the first instance this was to classify the varied terminology used at that time in the field, and then to see whether any cohesion could be found in the multiplicity of educational phenomena encountered. The bulk of the literature analysed was in English, but the considerable literature in German was not ignored. Efforts were made to gather literature in French and Spanish as well, although the results were relatively meagre.

Stage 2

Distance education, however, does not exist in a vacuum: it has been in action for over a hundred years. It was imperative, therefore, to see and participate in the institutions concerned.

Visits were carried out to sixty-two institutions that had been encountered in the literature. Included were structures large and small, public and private in Australia, India, the United Kingdom, Netherlands, Italy, Ireland, France, Germany, Hungary, Canada and the United States of America.

The institutions ranged from correspondence schools at primary and secondary levels to open universities. Some were eliminated from the study at a later date as being general non-traditional programmes rather than a part of distance education as it came to be defined.

The institutional studies were structured around a framework for the analysis of distance education institutions developed specially for the study (see Chapter 11).

Stage 3

Initial hypotheses about the nature and structure of the group-ings of educational phenomena encountered in the literature were constantly refined by feedback from the institutional case-studies. This led to a period of synthesis in which patterns and hypotheses were developed for the field as a whole.

Considerable care had to be exercised at this stage because of anomalies which had been discerned between the literature search and the institutional case-studies. With reference to the choice of non-print media, especially broadcast television, it quickly became evident that a disturbing amount of published research was exaggerated or inaccurate and that some of the researchers appeared not to have visited the institutions, nor even the countries, on which they were reporting.

As a result of this analysis an attempt was made to clarify the conceptual structure and terminology of the field in an article 'On defining distance education'. A first sketch of the field as a whole was published in Germany under the title *On the Nature of Distance Education*. This provoked further feedback both in pub-lished work and in private communications.

Stage 4

As a final stage more extensive visits of up to three months in length were undertaken to a number of the institutions in Eur-ope and North America which had emerged as central to the concept of the foundations of distance education.

INITIAL FINDINGS

As the work progressed it became clear that systemic similarities of a marked kind were present in all the institutions that fell within the definition of distance education being formulated. These similarities were the more remarkable as they cut sharply across the sectoral boundaries within which education is normally administered. They were characteristic of government primary and secondary correspondence schools, of private foundations (whether non-profit or profit-oriented), of government distance technical or further education colleges, and of open universities. Among these characteristics were:

- the absence of classrooms, lecture rooms, seminar rooms, and tutorial rooms;
- the presence of, or access to, comprehensive printing and materials production facilities;
- the absence of a library, or of places for student study, if there was a library;
- the central location of the warehouse;
- the absence of cafeterias, playgrounds, recreation facilities, drama and music amenities;
- the use of buildings which often resembled industrial offices, warehouses, or factories; and
- the fact that many of the institutions acted as post offices.

These divergences marked the institutions off from institutions structured for conventional, oral, group-based education in a striking and decisive way. In the case of a distance education department of an existing college or university, many of the characteristics noted were present, other things being equal, in the distance wing of the conventional institution. Here was a largely unstudied grouping of educational institutions, globally represented and growing in influence annually.

ANALYTICAL MODEL

The study had not been in progress long before it became clear that as a theoretical focus for the whole area of education being investigated, the 1973 thesis by Peters *Die didaktische Struktur des Fernunterrichts. Untersuchungen zu einer industrialisierten Form des Lehrens und Lernens* (The Didactical Structure of Distance Teaching. Investigations into a more Industrialized Form of Teaching and Learning) was by far the most satisfactory explanation yet formulated. Peters' comparative research on distance institutions of all types throughout the 1960s led to his characterization of distance education as 'the most industrialised form of education'.

18

The conclusions of his study surprised many researchers who recoiled from the implications of the position that his comparative and theoretical analysis led him to enunciate:

Anyone professionally involved in education is compelled to presume the existence of two forms of instruction which are strictly separable; traditional face-to-face teaching based on interpersonal communication and industrialised teaching which is based on an objectivised, rationalised, technologically-based interaction.

[Peters 1973: 313]

Peters had previously (1971) complained that the normal procedures of educational research had proved of little avail in the investigations of correspondence education:

Correspondence instruction is the most industrialised form of instruction and the usual theoretical criteria for the description of traditional instruction do not help very much in analysing correspondence instruction. [This] has suggested the introduction of new categories taken from those sciences investigating the industrial production process. It is, in fact, astounding to see how much better these criteria help to understand and describe the instructional process.

[Peters 1971: 225]

FEEDBACK MODEL

It might be appropriate, therefore, to investigate the phenomenon of distance education by a methodology more widely used in industrial situations. Such a methodology is available in control theory, which presents a coherent set of strategies for arriving at a prescribed goal.

Control theory is normally applied to systems that are a good deal simpler than educational research systems (Sparkes 1980); nevertheless it has valuable insights to offer. Control theory deals with what are called open-loop systems and closed-loop systems.

An open-loop system (Figure 1.1) differs from a closed-loop system in that it does not contain a feedback path from output to input. The goal, namely knowledge from educational research, is obtained as far as practicable by ensuring that the inputs are

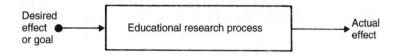

Figure 1.1 Educational research as an open-loop system
Source: Adapted from Belove and Drossman (1976)

correct and the system is well designed. An open-loop system is appropriate where facts rather than ideas or concepts are being researched because a good deal of knowledge can be attained by uncomplicated research. Nevertheless, as a research paradigm for distance education a closed-loop system with negative feedback is recommended.

A key concept in control theory is negative feedback. Most human activity is controlled by negative feedback loops (Sparkes 1980: 12). When one writes, speaks, walks, or plays football, one watches or listens to what is happening and uses this information to control what one does. Used as a paradigm for educational research, feedback theory draws attention to the benefits to be had when errors and inadequacies are pointed out and dealt with in a way that is likely to lead to their correction.

Negative feedback processes in educational research exemplify the conversational theory of human learning in that they underline that knowledge from research is achieved by a continuous iteration of the process of absorbing new information, trying to use it and then checking whether it was correctly used. In a feedback model concepts are recycled through the research process and gradually acquire sufficient richness of meaning for them to be used with confidence to express the researcher's findings.

Figure 1.2 illustrates a simple closed-loop system with negative feedback. This is a control system and the process is the educational research activity. The system input sets the goal which is the desired effect from the research. Crucial to such systems is the measurement or assessment of performance. The overall performance of the system is dominated by the effectiveness of the feedback path. By applying negative feedback in different ways it is possible to remove discrepancies and so enable the researcher to achieve the goal with greater accuracy.

In practical systems feedback paths and controllers are

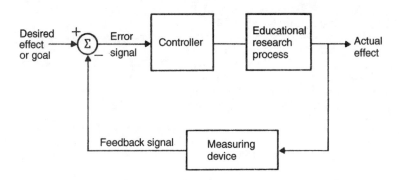

Figure 1.2 Educational research as a closed-loop system with negative feedback
Source: Adapted from Belove and Drossman (1976)

normally non-human and work automatically, whereas in educational research the controller is a human researcher. Thus, such models are essentially paradigms; that is, aids to the understanding of complex behaviour patterns.

Control theory provides a satisfactory methodology for the study of the phenomenon of distance education. It is synergistic, does not destroy the complexity of reality, and can encapsulate experience and common sense. Such a method can help in finding patterns in the complex reality of the world of distance systems and can provide guides for analysis. In this book educational research is seen as a closed-loop system with negative feedback.

REFERENCES

Bates, A.W. (1995) *Technology, Open Learning and Distance Education*, London: Routledge.

Belove, C. and Drossman, M. (1976) *Systems and Circuits for Electrical Engineering Technology*, New York: McGraw-Hill.

Childs, G. (1963) 'Supervised correspondence instruction', in *The Brandenburg Memorial Essays on Correspondence Instruction*, Madison: University of Wisconsin.

Coombs, P. (1978) *The World Crisis in Education*, Oxford: Oxford University Press.

Daniel, J. (1995) 'Preface' in F. Lockwood (ed.) *Open and Distance Learning Today*, London: Routledge.

Delling, R. (1966) 'Versuch der Grundlegung zu einer systematischen

Theorie des Fernunterrichts', in L. Sroka (ed.) *Fernunterricht 1966*, Hamburg: Hamburger Fernlehrinstitut.

Dohmen, G. (1967) *Das Fernstudium: Ein neues pädagogisches Forschungs- und Arbeitsfeld*, Tübingen: DIFF.

Garrison, D. (1985) 'Three generations of technological innovation in distance education', *Distance Education*, 6(2), 235–41.

Gough, E. (1984) 'Towards a philosophy of distance education', in K.Smith (ed.) *Diversity Down Under in Distance Education*, Toowoomba: Darling Downs Institute.

Graff, K. (1964) 'Briefwechsel und soziale Distanz', *Epistolodidaktika*, 1(1), 30–5.

Holmberg, B. (1960) *On the Methods of Teaching by Correspondence*, Lund: Gleerup.

Keegan, D. (1994) *Distance Training in the European Union*, Hagen: ZIFF.

Moore, M. (1973) 'Towards a theory of independent learning and teaching', *Journal of Higher Education*, 44, 666–78.

Moore, M. (1995a) 'American distance education: a short literature review', in F. Lockwood (ed.) *Open and Distance Learning Today*, London: Routledge.

Moore, M. (1995b) 'The 1995 Distance Education Research Symposium: a research agenda', *The American Journal of Distance Education* 9(2), 1–6.

Nipper, S. (1989) 'Third generation distance learning and computer conferencing', in R. Mason and A. Kaye, *Mindweave: Communication, Computers and Distance Education*, Oxford: Pergamon.

Peters, O.(1965) *Der Fernunterricht*, Basel: Weinheim.

Peters, O. (1971) 'Theoretical aspects of correspondence instruction', in O. Mackenzie and E. Christensen (eds) *The Changing World of Correspondence Study*, University Park: Pennsylvania State University.

Peters, O. (1973) *Die didaktische Struktur des Fernunterrichts. Untersuchungen zu einer industrialisierten Form des Lehrens und Lernens*, Weinheim: Beltz.

Peters, O. (1991) 'Towards a better understanding of distance education: analysing designations and catchwords', in B. Holmberg and G. Ortner (eds) *Research into Distance Education*, Frankfurt: Lang.

Portway P. and Lane, C. (1994) *Guide to Teleconferencing and Distance Learning*, San Ramon Calif.:Applied Business Telecommunications.

Rebel, K.-H. (1971) 'Die Funkkollegs der Quadriga', *Fernsehen und Bildung*, 3, 185–94.

Sparkes, J. (1980) *Feedback Theory* (Technology Foundation course unit No. 1), Milton Keynes: Open University.

Sparkes, J. (1983) 'The problem of creating a discipline of distance education', *Distance Education* 4(2), 197–205.

Wedemeyer, C. (1963) 'Problems of learning by correspondence' in *The Brandenburg Memorial Essays on Correspondence Instruction*, Madison: University of Wisconsin.

Wedemeyer, C. (1981) *Learning at the Back-door*, Madison: University of Wisconsin.

Wei, R. and Tong, Y. (1994) *Radio and TV Universities: The Mainstream of China's Adult and Distance Higher Education*, Nanjing: Jilin Press.

2

OPEN, NON-TRADITIONAL AND DISTANCE EDUCATION

When we studied the research in education we read, for example, that . . . 'the word instruction refers to the activity which takes place during schooling, and within the CLASS-ROOM setting'. It was clear that a vast number of adult learners were receiving instruction in non-group settings, and we concluded that educational theory which did not provide a place for such learning and teaching was incomplete, and unsatisfactory.

Michael G. Moore, 1971

BACKGROUND

When the research reported in this book began, analysis of distance education was characterized by confusion over terminology and by lack of precision on what areas of education were being discussed or what was being excluded. The result was discourtesy to the reader and fragility of the field of study.

The confusion can be highlighted by listing the terms used in English for this field of education: 'correspondence study', 'home study', 'external studies', 'independent study', 'teaching at a distance', 'off-campus study', 'open learning' – and there may well have been more.

Allied to this was inconsistency about the boundaries that could be set to areas that had some similarities to distance education, either in philosophy or procedure, but which could not be identified with it. Writers did not make it clear when they used the term 'distance education' whether they were writing about or not writing about the use of computers in schools or educational broadcasting or rural development projects or technology-based training. Similarly in the period 1990–5 there is considerable imprecision in the use of 'distance education', 'open learning', 'flexible learning', 'open and distance learning', and, even, 'open distance learning'.

The purpose of this chapter is to underline the importance of clarity for the didactical analyst. Its importance lies in the fact that the meanings we choose to use for things and how we and others conceive of things (here 'distance education') subtly but surely direct the actions that we and others take. The purpose is heuristic and not managerial. Educational managers will choose programmes to suit students and may wish to blur the boundaries between them. But for progress in the study of distance education it is important to provide in this chapter an analysis of forms of non-conventional education which may have similarities to distance education but are not to be identified with it. The next chapter then attempts to define distance education in a way which identifies it and isolates it for heuristic purposes from other forms of education.

METHODOLOGY

The research began with an analysis of a very large grouping of institutions that had non-conventional or distance elements. The list included public and private correspondence schools, rural development projects, educational broadcasting networks, open colleges and universities, external and distance departments of conventional institutions, universities without walls, extramural and external degree programmes, experiential learning and other experimental structures.

The findings confirmed the results of an investigation of 'more than 2,000 items of literature pertaining to educational programmes in which learners were not in face-to-face relationships with teachers', carried out by Moore at the University of Wisconsin a decade earlier. Moore presents the result of his investigation thus: 'Teaching consists of two families of activity with many characteristics in common, but different in one aspect so important that a theory explaining one cannot satisfactorily explain the other' (1977: 5).

Moore describes his two families of educational activities:

- The first of these families, the older, better understood, more fully researched, includes all educational situations where the teacher is physically contiguous with his students, so that the primary means of communication is his voice, and in which (to use the economists' terms) teaching is a 'service' that is 'consumed' simultaneously with its 'production'.
- The second family of teaching methods, and the subject of our concern, includes educational situations distinguished by the separation of the teacher from his learners, so that communication has to be facilitated by a mechanical or electronic medium. Teaching in this environment is 'consumed' at a time or place different from that at which it is 'produced', and to reach the learner it must be contained, transported, stored and delivered. There may be interaction, between learner and teacher, but if so, it is so greatly affected by the delay resulting from the necessity to communicate across distance or time, that it cannot be an assured component of teaching strategy, as it may in classroom or group teaching. We refer to this as *Distance Teaching*.

(Moore 1977: 6)

The field of study known as conventional education is first briefly described and then the concepts 'non-traditional education', 'open learning', and 'flexible learning' are considered and the characteristics of the fields of adult education and educational technology are described.

CONVENTIONAL EDUCATION

Moore's 'first family of education activities' is often referred to as 'conventional education'. Conventional education is the normal on-campus provision at school, college, or university level. For the purposes of this book the description provided by Kaye and Rumble is adequate: 'The term "conventional education" is applied to formal classroom-based instruction in a school, college, or university setting, where teacher and students are physically present at the same time at the same place' (1979: 22).

In educational literature this is regarded as the 'normal' form of educational provision and the complaint of Moore that he had found hundreds of references of the type 'the word instruction refers to the activity which takes place during schooling, and within the classroom setting' could be made with little variation in the late 1990s. Distance education still merits not a paragraph in most volumes of educational philosophy, in guides to administrative practice and in analyses of didactic strategy. A major justification for this is that society has for some hundreds, if not thousands, of years provided itself with locations called 'schools' and higher-level locations called 'universities' to which students travel or at which students reside for the purposes of instruction. Distance education students choose not to travel to these institutions and prefer to remain at home, or – as in the Chinese system – at their workplace. They now expect to be provided with instruction at home and, more and more frequently in the 1990s, receive university degrees at home.

In distance education writing, one often finds the term 'face-to-face education' used for normal provision. In this book an attempt at further precision is made with the use from time to time of the term 'conventional, oral, group-based education' in place of 'face-to-face'.

NON-TRADITIONAL EDUCATION

The relationship between non-traditional education and distance education was addressed by Moore in the early 1970s when he considered that distance education formed part of non-traditional education (1971: 661). This allocation would contribute to the fragility of this form of education and its continued lack of status in the eyes of many administrators and educationists in conventional institutions.

Van den Brande, writing in 1993, states that 'until relatively recently such provision had often been regarded as a second-best alternative to conventional education'. Does this remain true in the late 1990s? The beginnings of an answer are provided by Perry, the foundation vice-chancellor of the Open University of the United Kingdom:

Academics all over Britain accept that the Open University has succeeded, that distance learning works and that the Open University graduates are as good as any others. They (these graduates) have been accepted by every other British university in postgraduate courses without question. The quality of the courses is seen and is commended by the academics in other universities. But, emotionally many of them don't accept it at all. Emotionally, there still is a strong feeling that on-campus teaching in the face-to-face situation is the one way of actually teaching and that this is the vital thing in order to train scholars for the future. It may take decades rather than years to overcome this emotional reaction.

(Perry 1986: 15)

Central to overcoming these barriers to acceptance are the solid grounding of the foundations of distance education and the formulation of guides to good practice.

OPEN EDUCATION

There is extensive overlap between the use of the term 'open education' and distance education. The decision of the United Kingdom government in the mid-1960s to rename the 'University of the Air' the 'Open University' popularized the term 'open'. It is found in the titles of the distance teaching universities in Pakistan, Sri Lanka, Thailand and Venezuela. Keegan and Rumble (1982: 12) argued that the open universities should be more correctly termed 'distance teaching universities' but the prestige of the Open University was too strong and the most recent foundations all used the term 'open': the Open University of Tanzania (1993), the Open University of Bangladesh (1994) and the Open University of Catalonia (1995).

There was widespread interest in 'open' education and 'open' learning in the United States in the 1960s and in the United Kingdom in the 1980s, and the term is widely used in the late 1990s (Kember 1995). McKenzie *et al.* in their 1975 book *Open Learning* define 'open learning' as follows:

Open learning is an imprecise phrase to which a range of meanings can be, and is, attached. It eludes definition. But as an inscription to be carried in procession on a banner, gathering adherents and enthusiasms, it has great potential. For its very imprecision enables it to accommodate many different ideas and aims.

(McKenzie *et al.* 1975: 21)

They showed that the two terms of the phrase 'open learning' carry with them emotional overtones that evoke a wide response: educationists wish to be 'open' rather than closed; 'learning' supports student-centredness rather than teacher-centredness. (Delling 1994).

'Open' learning, however, is a term that is used with difficulty in an administrative context; its context is, rather, theoretical and describes, for instance, colleges with 'open' administration policies or a special spirit. Open learning can, in fact, be carried on under both face-to-face and distance conditions. Many of the distance teaching universities, for instance, have closed and rigid structures, are inflexible and slow to respond to community education needs, have cut-off dates for computer-marked assignments and fixed assessment patterns. They design learning materials that narrow the curriculum and leave little room for interpretation outside the direction provided by the course designers. Thus, while some basic ideas are shared by both open learning and distance education, the terms are not synonymous.

The mid-1980s to the mid-1990s saw rapid development of open learning in the United Kingdom. One of the largest providers is Manchester Open Learning from the Manchester College of Arts and Technology. Its schemes vary in the amount and forms of attendance they require. The basic model is that of corporate management training providers who give resource-based in-company training with freelance tutors who work in the company for in-depth sessions on an occasional basis.

The difficulties with the term 'open learning' is that people vary in what they call 'open': many of the distance systems studies in this book have open admission dates; most of the open universities do not. Plato is generally praised for opening the world to philosophy and for the openness of his dialogue system of education; he was bitterly criticized by Popper (1960) for being closed in *The Open Society and its Enemies*. The terms 'open teaching' and 'open education' have had a less-wide usage than 'open learning'.

In any case distance education is neither open nor closed, it is just a form of education. Many distance courses are closed because the course authors close off all other views or interpretations besides the one chosen for presentation, or because they have closed enrolment procedures or closed cut-off dates for assignment submission or close out students who cannot attend compulsory group meetings. Rumble sums it up well by saying that the values of openness 'have nothing intrinsically to do with distance education which is morally ambivalent (i.e. it can promote open learning or closed learning)' (Rumble 1991: 72). Rumble is right: distance education is just a form of educational provision. It is quite neutral. Some courses are open, some are closed; *per se* it is neither.

It is felt, therefore, that the terms 'open learning' and 'distance education' can be adequately distinguished in spite of the practice, especially in the United Kingdom, Australia, Denmark and elsewhere, to blur the distinctions between them.

FLEXIBLE LEARNING

Closely allied to the concept 'open learning' is the concept 'flexible learning'. Van den Brande calls her study for the European Union in Brussels *Flexible and Distance Learning*. She defines 'flexible learning' as:

> Enabling learners to learn when they want (frequency, timing, duration), how they want (modes of learning), and what they want (that is learners can define what constitutes learning to them). These flexible learning principles may be applied at a distance. If so then the term 'distance learning' is used. In such cases the learners can choose where they want to learn (at home, at an institution or company, at a training centre, etc.)
>
> (Van den Brande 1993: 2)

The choice of this terminology may indicate a desire to move on from the vagueness of 'open learning' or 'open and 'distance learning' to 'flexible learning' and 'flexible and distance learning'. Similarly, in Australia one can see a movement from External Studies in the early 1990s to Distance Educational Centres, and then to Open Learning Networks and to Flexible Learning Centres by the mid-1990s.

For this study distance education is a form of education. It is neither flexible nor inflexible *per se* and it seems impossible scientifically to decide whether an open university course with 10 CMAs and 15 TMAs is flexible or inflexible, or whether it would be more flexible or less flexible with a different structure.

ADULT EDUCATION

Distance education as a field for academic study started some 150 years ago, has clearly defined boundaries at the time of writing, and is studied as a subject in some university degree programmes at bachelors, masters and doctorate levels. It has affinities to other fields of study within the discipline education: notably, adult education and educational technology.

Moore (1985) guessed that the study of distance education had reached the level of development that the field of the study of adult education had reached thirty years previously. This is a useful yardstick, probably not too far wide of the mark.

The fields of teaching and research known as adult education and distance education have a number of distinguishing characteristics:

- adult education deals with the education of adults; distance education is the study of the education of children and adults at a distance and theoretical positions in this field must be equally valid for children as for adults;
- adult group dynamics as the basis of the 'andragogical' approach to adult education would be excluded by definition from most approaches to distance education;
- the eighty-year history of children's distance education has provided an essential database for distance education research (children do not, for instance, drop out of distance education systems);
- experiences with educating children at a distance are particularly notable in Australia, Canada, France and New Zealand;
- children's distance education has been the impetus for important distance education innovations such as the Star Schools Project in the USA in the mid-1990s (Cabrara-Herrenan 1994).

Although it is true that a large percentage of students enrolled in distance education programmes worldwide are adults, from the point of view of the analyst and the theorist all positions established must be equally valid for children studying at a distance as for adults.

EDUCATIONAL TECHNOLOGY

Educational technology is the field of study that analyses the use of technology in education (Hawkridge 1976). Its findings are directed primarily at schools, colleges and universities, but are of central interest to distance systems as well because of the crucial importance of technology in these systems. Among the differences of focus and of emphasis in the two fields of study are:

- in distance education face-to-face group-based communication is absent either wholly or substantially; educational technology does not abandon interpersonal communication: it nourishes and supports it;
- educational technology deals with the use of technology for the education of 600 million students in the world; distance education does not have this role;
- distance education is a form of education in which millions of students are enrolled annually in a vast array of subjects and courses with different enrolment criteria and examination structures; educational technology does not have these characteristics;
- distance education is a form of education; education technology is a field of educational research;
- in distance education, the technology is a substitute for the teacher; in educational technology the technology is a supplement to the teacher;
- distance education studies the problems of students who learn at home or at the office, for whom face-to-face group-based communication is entirely, or to a large extent, absent. Educational technology does not in any way abandon face-to-face group-based communication. It does in fact presume face-to-face interaction as the basis for interpretation of the technology.

REFERENCES

Cabrara-Herrenan, P. (1994) 'Distance learning: K through 12', in P. Portway and C. Lane (eds) *Guide to Teleconferencing and Distance Learning*, San Ramon, Calif.: Applied Business Communications.

Delling, R. (1994) 'Offenes Lernen – ein Literaturbericht', pp. 191–226 in G. Zimmer (ed.) *Vom Fernunterricht zum Open Distance Learning*, Berlin: BIBB.

Hawkridge, D. (1976) 'Next year Jerusalem! The rise of educational technology', *British Journal of Educational Technology* 7(1), 7–30.

Kaye, A. and Rumble, G. (1979) *An Analysis of Distance Teaching Systems*, Milton Keynes: Open University.

Keegan, D. and Rumble, G (1982) 'Distance teaching at university level', in G. Rumble and K. Harry (eds) *The Distance Teaching Universities*, London: Croom Helm.

Kember, D. (1995) *Open Learning Courses for Adults. A Model of Student Progress*, Englewood Cliffs: Educational Technology Publications.

McKenzie, O., Postgate, R. and Scupham, J. (eds) *(1975) Open Learning*, Paris: Unesco.

Moore, M. (1971) 'Toward a theory of independent learning and teaching', *Journal of Higher Education* 44, 661–79.

Moore, M. (1977) *On a Theory of Independent Study*, Hagen: Fernuniversität (ZIFF).

Moore, M. (1985) 'Some observations on current research in distance education', *Epistolodidaktika* 1, 35–62.

Perry, W. (1986) 'Distance education, trends worldwide', pp. 15–20 in G. van Enckevort *et al.* (eds) *Distance Education and the Adult Learner*, Heerlen: Open Universiteit.

Popper, K. (1960) *The Open Society and its Enemies*, London: Macmillan.

Rumble, G. (1991) 'Book review', *Open Learning*, February, 71–2.

Van den Brande, L. (1993) *Flexible and Distance Learning*, Chichester: Wiley.

3

DEFINITION OF DISTANCE EDUCATION

It is natural for man to desire to know.

Aristotle, 323 BC

CONTEXT

The purpose of this chapter is to enable readers to make their way through the terminology encountered in the literature, and then to formulate a definition of the area of education under study as a basis for discussion in this book. The definition developed here may then be used by analysts as an instrument to identify forms of educational provision which should be included in a study of distance education and to identify forms which should be excluded, although they show similarities to it. The methodology used is based on the contributions of established experts in the field coupled with the use of feedback techniques.

One of the advantages of seeing educational research in the context of feedback techniques is that it solves the problem of which comes first: the research or the hypothesis. In feedback theory, investigation is seen as a loop process and one can commence at any appropriate point in the loop in the attempt to deepen knowledge and understanding.

A DESCRIPTION

The need to clarify terminology in this field is urgent. No progress can be made in formulating the theoretical underpinnings of an area of educational endeavour or in developing guides to good practice if there is not agreement on the area of education under discussion.

This book proposes the adoption of 'distance education' as a generic term for the field of education under analysis. It may be described thus: 'Distance education' is a generic term that includes the range of teaching/learning strategies used by correspondence colleges, open universities, distance departments of conventional colleges or universities and distance training units of corporate providers. It is a term for the education of those who choose not to attend the schools, colleges and universities of the world but study at their home, or sometimes their workplace. In French it is referred to as *enseignement* or *formation à distance*, *Fernstudium/Fernunterricht* in German, *educación a distancia* in Spanish and *istruzione a distanza* in Italian.

This description lists the major providers of distance education and gives parallel terms for the major European languages and acts as the basis for the literature and institutional analyses in this part of the study. From the outset it can be seen that this form of education crosses the sectoral boundaries into which the study of education is normally divided, with major points of focus on:

- children's education at a distance;
- further education at a distance for vocational qualifications (distance training);
- higher education at a distance for university qualifications (university-level distance education);
- corporate distance training (in-house courses in which the public may not be invited to enrol).

A complete title for the field would, therefore, be 'distance education and training'. 'Distance education' is used as a shorter form of this.

TERMINOLOGY

The term 'distance education' subsumes a number of existing terms but not all are synonymous. The terms considered here have been used from time to time as generic for the field as a whole.

Correspondence education/correspondence study

These terms have a long history in the education of children and adults at a distance. They still have their supporters who claim that much distance education is still organized through the post and that both the public and prospective students recognize the terms. It is used today by the Association of European Correspondence Schools (AECS) in its title and in 1994 over 75 per cent of distance education provision in Europe was in the distance training area in which the association is a major player. The association, however, also uses the term 'distance education' and calls its professional qualification the AECS Diploma in Distance Education and its journal *Epistolodidaktika: the European Journal of Distance Education.*

The main difficulty with the term 'correspondence education' is that it cannot encompass the didactic potential of this form of education in the 1990s and beyond: print-, audio-, video-, and computer-based technologies must be reflected by the terminology chosen. Critics of the term tend to associate 'correspondence education' and 'correspondence study' with some of the less successful aspects of distance education in the past and feel that these terms contribute to the still-questioned status of study at a distance in some countries.

A term is, however, needed to designate the postal sub-group of the print-based forms of distance education in which compulsory or voluntary meetings are not felt necessary. It seems suitable to reserve the term 'correspondence education' for this purpose.

Home study

In 1926 when the directors of the correspondence schools of the United States came together to form an association, the title chosen was the National Home Study Council. In 1995 its members enrolled 5 million students.

The term was used in the United States for further education at a distance (technical and vocationally orientated institutions) but not for higher education (universities and university-oriented colleges). One of the difficulties in using 'home study' as a generic term is that the distance student may not, in fact, study at home or may study in part at home and in part at other centres. In 1994 the association was renamed the Council for Distance Education and Training.

Independent study

The major proponent of 'independent study' as an overall term for this area of education was Charles A. Wedemeyer, formerly of the University of Wisconsin at Madison. Wedemeyer considered that 'Independent study in the American context is generic for a range of teaching–learning activities that sometimes go by separate names (correspondence study, open education, radio–television teaching, individualised learning)' (1977: 2115).

This term is often used for distance education programmes at higher education level in the US (Markowitz 1983). Its weakness as a generic term is that it indicates independence from an educational institution and this is not the case in distance education. In 1995 in the United States the term is still widely used for university-level distance education programmes.

External studies

'External studies' was the term most widely used in Australia. it describes well the ethos of distance education as found in Australian universities and colleges of advanced education: a form of education that is 'external to' but not 'separated from' the faculty staff of the institution. The same staff have two groups of students, one on-campus, the other external, and they prepare both groups for the same examinations and awards.

In the early 1990s External Studies departments of Australian universities were renamed Distance Education Centres and the Australian association changed its name to the Open and Distance Learning Association of Australia.

Distance teaching or teaching at a distance

These two terms have been used as a characteristic of this form of education for many years. Moore described 'distance teaching' as:

> All those teaching methods in which, because of the physical separation of learners and teachers, the interactive

36

(simulation, explanation, questioning, guidance) as well as the proactive phase of teaching (selecting objectives, planning curriculum and instructional strategies), is conducted through print, mechanical or electronic devices.

(Moore 1973: 669)

The term has grown greatly in popularity since the development of the Open University (UK) which used it for its didactic strategies. It is, nevertheless, inadequate for the field of education we want to define. Just as 'distance learning' would be too student-based as an overall term and would tend to ignore the role of the institution, so 'distance teaching' is too teacher-oriented and places all the emphasis on the institution.

Distance learning or learning at a distance

In the 1990s the term 'distance learning' has grown in usage. Many authors use it in an administrative sense or for the field as a whole. This emphasizes the student-centredness of the process, with 'distance education' being regarded as too bureaucratic and 'distance teaching' too teacher-centred. In this study, however, phrases like 'the funding of distance learning' are regarded as metaphorical, as learning is considered to be internal to the student. Governments can support open or distance education; they can fund open or distance teaching but they cannot cause learning to occur.

In the United States the term 'distance learning' has come to be used as a global term for the use of electronic technologies in distance education. Portway and Lane (1994) use it to cover audioconferencing, audiographics, teleconferencing, business television (one-way video teaching by satellite), videoconferencing, two-way interactive video and also desktop videoconferencing.

In this book 'distance learning' is used for the learning half of the distance education process and not for the field as a whole.

Distance education

Distance teaching and distance learning are each only half the process we are seeking to describe. 'Distance teaching' indicates well the process of course development by which a distance institution prepares learning materials for students. In the same way wide currency has been given to the term 'distance learning' or 'learning at a distance' for the process as seen from the student's perspective. There is a peculiar necessity in distance systems that the perspective of student learning, as well as distance teaching, should be encompassed within the term chosen. 'Distance teaching' often does not teach. Costly distance teaching materials, prepared over months and sometimes years, often lie unopened and discarded in the homes of prospective students. The essential intersubjectivity that has often been seen as the essence of the education process has not occurred.

'Distance education' is a suitable term to bring together both the teaching and learning elements of this field of education. The relationship of 'distance teaching' and 'distance learning' may be illustrated as shown in Figure 3.1.

Figure 3.1 Relationship of distance teaching to distance education

Since the early 1980s the term 'distance education' has gained in strength and acceptance. It indicates well the basic characteristic of this form of education: the separation of teacher and learner which distinguishes it from conventional, oral, group-based education. It also encompasses well the two characteristic operating systems which later in this study will be shown to be characteristic of distance education: the course development subsystem (distance teaching) and a student support subsystem (distance learning).

It is also a term for the future. Distance educators in the past have held on to terms like 'correspondence' or 'home study' because, it was claimed, they were comforting to students. There is every evidence that citizens of the late 1990s will be able to cope with distance in a way previous generations could never dream of. Students, too, are coming to choose distance rather than backing off from it.

Perhaps the main problem with the term is that it tends to mask the fact that many students in distance systems are metropolitan residents and that it is the distance between the teaching acts and the learning acts that is crucial, not the magnitude of the geographical separation of teacher and learner.

In this chapter 'distance education' is chosen as the most suitable term for this form of education and it is proposed as the only term for international usage. Terms that are considered synonymous with or constituents of it were discussed earlier in this chapter; terms for fields of education or educational strategies that are similar to it but not to be regarded as synonymous with it were discussed in Chapter 2.

A DEFINITION OF DISTANCE EDUCATION

A clear idea of what is the subject of discussion is essential in a book on an area of study in which there has been much confusion about terminology. A clear definition is also important in the rather ill-defined areas of non-traditional education, open education, and flexible education. It is important to be able to say whether distance education is to be regarded as the same as or different from a university without walls, extramural studies, experiential learning, off-campus education, open learning, extended campus, the American external degree, or university extension.

The rest of this chapter seeks to establish a definition of distance education which will serve as a basis for the analysis in the rest of the book.

A satisfactory framework for definition in education is provided by the American educational philosopher Scheffler (1968), who presented the scheme shown in Figure 3.2 for classifying different types of definition. Scheffler sees *scientific definitions* as being based on special knowledge which is used to construct a network of theory adequate to all available facts encompassed in the definition, whereas *general definitions* are statements that a given term is to be understood in a certain way for the space of some discussions or for several discussions.

Scheffler claims there are three types of general definitions: stipulative, descriptive, and programmatic. Stipulative definitions state that a given term is to be taken as equivalent to some other given term within a particular context. This is not the type of definition needed here, as a stipulative definition does not claim

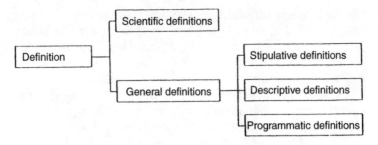

Figure 3.2 Types of definition in education
Source: Adapted from Scheffler (1968)

to reflect the previously accepted usage of the defined term. A general descriptive definition answers the question 'What does that term mean?' It not only serves as a convention for usage in discussion but also always explains the defined term by giving an account of its prior usage. A programmatic definition is a definition with a purpose, a programme: it seeks to include additional items within a term or to exclude from a term elements which people had previously thought were included.

In Scheffler's terms this study commences with a general descriptive definition and seeks to proceed by feedback and refinement towards a scientific definition of distance education.

It seems appropriate to begin with a search of the literature for authoritative or accepted definitions and to analyse them for their common elements. Distance education, however, has a history which spans a hundred years and more, and the elements of a definition that can be established by this process do not therefore exist as abstractions; they must correspond to the reality.

It is proposed, therefore, to examine the definition being developed in the context of existing institutions, then to consider more recent definitions before re-examining the definition established in the light of existing institutions. The process is then continued: it is cyclic and continuous. If the search of the literature is extensive and if the case-studies of institutions to which the nascent definition is applied are wide and varied, it should be possible within the confines of this chapter to produce a definition instrument capable of delineating all educational institutions either into the category 'distance education' and hence subjects within the scope of this book, or of excluding them and therefore to regard them as the subject of other studies.

EARLY DEFINITIONS

G. Dohmen (1967)

The first definition is chosen from Dohmen, a director of the German Distance Education Institute (DIFF) at Tübingen.

> Distance education *(Fernstudium)* is a systematically organized form of self-study in which student counselling, the presentation of learning material and the securing and supervising of students' success is carried out by a team of teachers, each of whom has responsibilities. It is made possible at a distance by means of media which can cover long distances. The opposite of 'distance education' is 'direct education' or 'face-to-face education': a type of education that takes place with direct contact between lecturers and students.
>
> (Dohmen 1967: 9)

O. Peters (1973)

Peters worked at the DIFF in Tübingen and then at the Fernuniversität in Hagen.

> Distance teaching/education *(Fernunterricht)* is a method of imparting knowledge, skills and attitudes which is rationalized by the application of division of labour and organizational principles as well as by the extensive use of technical media, especially for the purpose of reproducing high quality teaching material which makes it possible to instruct great numbers of students at the same time wherever they live. It is an industrialized form of teaching and learning.
>
> (Peters 1973: 206)

M. Moore (1973)

This definition is presented in 1973 and repeated without modification in 1977:

> Distance teaching may be defined as the family of instructional methods in which the teaching behaviours are executed apart from the learning behaviours, including those that in a contiguous situation would be performed in the

41

learner's presence, so that communication between the teacher and the learner must be facilitated by print, electronic, mechanical or other devices.

(Moore 1973: 664; 1977: 8)

B. Holmberg (1977)

Holmberg writes from a developed knowledge of the literature in English, German and the Scandinavian languages.

The term 'distance education' covers the various forms of study at all levels which are not under the continuous, immediate supervision of tutors present with their students in lecture rooms or on the same premises, but which, nevertheless, benefit from the planning, guidance and tuition of a tutorial organisation.

(Holmberg 1977: 9)

Analysis of these definitions leads to the recognition of certain common elements. The separation of teacher and learner is fundamental to all forms of distance education whether they be print-based, audio/radio-based, video/television-based, or computer-based. This separation differentiates distance education from all forms of conventional, face-to-face, direct teaching and learning. The structuring of learning materials and the linking of these learning materials to effective learning by students through an educational organization differentiates distance education from private study, learning from interesting books or cultural television programmes.

RECENT DEFINITIONS

Indicative of more recent efforts to define this area of education are:

D. Garrison and D. Shale (1987)

Distance education implies that the majority of educational communication between (among) teacher and student(s) occurs noncontiguously. It must involve two-way communication between (among) teacher and student(s) for the purpose of facilitating and supporting the educational process. It uses technology to mediate the necessary two-way communication.

(Garrison and Shale 1987: 11)

B. Barker and others (1989)

Barker and his colleagues argue for the broadening of the definition of distance education in the light of the new telecommunications technologies. They write:

Telecommunications-based distance education approaches are an extension beyond the limits of correspondence study. The teaching–learning experience for both instructor and student(s) occurs simultaneously – it is contiguous in time. When an audio and/or video communication link is employed, the opportunity for live teacher–student exchanges in real time is possible, thereby permitting immediate response to student inquiries and comments. Much like a traditional classroom setting, students can seek on-the-spot clarification from the speaker.

(Barker *et al.* 1989: 25)

M. Moore (1990)

Moore writes from Pennsylvania State University as editor of *The American Journal of Distance Education*.

Distance education is all arrangements for providing instruction through print or electronic communications media to persons engaged in planned learning in a place or time different from that of the instructor or instructors.

(Moore 1990: xv)

P. Portway and C. Lane (1994)

For their volume on telecommunications technologies in distance education Lane supplies:

The term 'distance education' refers to teaching and learning situations in which the instructor and the learner or learners are geographically separated, and therefore, rely on electronic devices and print materials for instructional delivery.

Distance education includes distance teaching – the instructor's role in the process – and distance learning – the student's role in the process.

(Lane 1994: 195)

TOWARDS A SYNTHESIS

In an article published in 1980, 'On defining distance education' (Keegan 1980), a number of similar definitions were brought together and analysed. Six basic defining elements of distance education were proposed:

- the separation of teacher and learner which distinguishes it from face-to-face lecturing;
- the influence of an educational organization which distinguishes it from private study;
- the use of technical media, usually print, to unite teacher and learner and carry the educational content;
- the provision of two-way communication so that the student may benefit from or even initiate dialogue;
- the possibility of occasional meetings for both didactic and socialization purposes; and
- the participation in an industrialized form of education which, if accepted, contains the genus of radical separation of distance education from other forms within the educational spectrum.

The publication of this definition in 1980 led to extensive citation and feedback. In some cases it seemed that the definition was accepted as the basis for further research; in others commentary was provided which might lead to further precision. Further analysis and case-studies of existing institutions led to the considerations which follow.

The separation of teacher and learner

An analysis of the definitions given in this chapter shows that the separation of teacher and learner is central to nearly all of them. This characteristic distinguishes distance education from conventional, oral, group-based education. Both the general public and educational writers appear to coincide in their acceptance of the separation of teacher and learner as a central characteristic of this

44

form of education. An examination of institutions revealed various levels of separation, in which contact with the teacher could range from nil, to voluntary, to compulsory, with varied theoretical justifications being given as to why face-to-face interaction in distance education should be nil, or optional to the learner, or imposed by the institution. 'Quasi-permanent separation throughout the length of the learning process' was finally chosen as a suitable overall summing up of the mean of practice.

The role of the educational organization

It is important to delineate distance education not only from what happens in lecture theatres and classrooms but also from private study at home. Distance education is an institutionalized offering through public or private providers. It is clear that people learn a lot throughout their lives, generally away from teachers and educational institutions. This may be from private reading, from TV, from attending a talk, from a friend, or in a thousand different ways. Distance education is an institutionalized form of provision. It shares with private study the individualized and private nature of study outside the structures of the learning group and at the same time has much of the administrative characteristics of institutionalized education on-campus.

Fieldwork in distance institutions shows that the entry of an educational bureaucracy into what appears to be a private form of education is not always without trauma.

The place of the technological medium (media)

In conventional systems the content of the course, especially that part that is not contained in recommended textbooks, is communicated by the teacher mainly by word of mouth – though it is clear that from primary school through to university the amount of self-study in project work and from textbooks may gradually increase. Distance education replaces this interpersonal communication with some form of mechanical or electronic communication: print, telephone, teleconference, audio, video, broadcasting, computer. All of the communication has to take place by the use of one or a number of technological media.

Many years ago Delling (1966: 173) called this element in a distance system the 'signal-carrier' and because of the diversity of procedures involved, careful formulation is needed of the role of the technological media in a definition of distance education.

Two-way communication

A definition of distance education needs to distinguish it from educational technology with which it is often confused. This can be accomplished neatly by defining that two-way communication is essential in distance education and showing its absence in educational technology.

It is important that the student in a distance system can profit from dialogue with the institution that provides the learning materials; the student should be able to initiate this dialogue and not be just the recipient of it. Two-way communication is not provided by the publishers of textbooks nor even of do-it-yourself books or their technological equivalents. Two-way communication is not possible with educational television or radio programmes like *Sesame Street* or 'Learn French at home by radio' nor even by video or audiocassettes produced as resource materials for lecture or classroom use.

The separation of learner and the learning group

In the 1980 definition the 'possibility of occasional seminars' was listed as one of the constituents of a definition of distance education. In the light of feedback and further research it has been found necessary to restructure this formulation. Some definitions of distance education tended to emphasize 'the teaching of students as individuals' and the importance of individualization in this form of education. Comparative research carried on after the publication of the 1980 definition, however, showed the survival in certain Scandinavian countries of group-based distance education (Edstrom *et al.* 1970). The presentation of individualization in the formulation of the definitions had, therefore, to be modified, as a prerequisite for the methodology adopted was that all the evidence should be reflected.

Further feedback from Garrison and Shale (1987: 9), Sparkes (1987: 237) and others made it important to emphasize the role in distance education of electronic groupings of students, by audioconferencing, teleconferencing, and computer conferences, in addition to the physical groupings reported by Edstrom *et al.*

It became clearer, moreover, that a focus on the study situation of the student was central to the concept of distance education. Some formula had to be found to reflect both the individualization of the distance student and the practice of institutions of providing either voluntary, compulsory, or non face-to-face sessions. The reason for this is that in most conventional educational institutions one has to join a learning group or class if one wants to enrol in a course. The presence of the learning group is as fundamental a characteristic of conventional education as the timetabling of classes so that the teacher and student can be present in the same place and at the same time.

Distance education is different in that it does not compel the student to join the learning group in order to study. Most distance systems treat the student basically as an individual; group work may be compulsory, optional, or may never occur, depending on the structure of the distance system in which one enrols. Some of the synchronous technologies introduced in the 1990s, however, like two-way or one-way video satellite or compressed video transmissions require the students to travel to electronic classrooms at fixed schedules to join a group of students.

The advantages and disadvantages of the absence of the learning group in distance education is an important area for future research. Together with the separation of the learner from the teacher, the separation of the learner from the learning group throughout the length of the learning process is a characteristic feature of most modes of this form of education and distinguishes it from conventional, oral, group-based structures. The absence of the learning group is best described as 'quasi-permanent': many systems have no meetings at all so that students are usually taught as individuals and not in groups, though physical or electronic meetings (audioconferences, videoconferences, computer-assisted conferences) feature in some systems.

SOCIAL ISSUES

Industrialization

The 1980 definition incorporated as an inherent characteristic an evaluation of Peters' industrialization theory. This decision was made after an analysis of the hundreds of institutional

case-studies presented by Peters in his study of distance education at technological and further education levels (Peters 1965)
and at higher education level (Peters 1968) in most countries of
the world, plus the analysis undertaken by the author of the
same or other institutions.

Reaction has been mixed. Some commentators, especially
those writing from a management or administrative perspective
(Rumble 1986) consider that Peters has provided a valuable
insight. Others (Bååth 1981; Willén 1981) have hesitated at the
harshness of Peters' terminology and doubted whether his concept of industrialization can be applied to all distance systems,
especially small correspondence schools.

The concept of the industrialization of teaching and learning
(see Chapter 5) has, none the less, proved to be a rich theme and
in 1995 there was extended debate on the relationship of distance education to industrialization, post-industrial society,
Fordism, post-Fordism and other contemporary philosophical
positions (Rumble 1995).

Privatization

Early definitions of distance education, especially those of
Wedemeyer and Moore, tended to emphasize the independence, autonomy, and freedom of the distance learner. There
are excellent elements in this concept but when it is compared
with the reality of existing systems, it can be shown to have
elements of Scheffler's programmatic type of definition in it. It
proposes a programme, an ideal. Many systems, in fact, do not
promote learner autonomy in the way this concept would wish.
Sharp cut-off dates for tutor-marked assignments (TMAs) and
computer-marked assignments (CMAs), rigidity of content of
learning materials, and inflexible learning structures are all too
common in distance systems.

Independence, therefore, is not the element that the definition
should reflect. The term 'privatization' is much closer to the
reality. A distance system takes the student from the learning
group and places him/her in a more private situation. Learning
is often private when it is not institutionalized. Distance education is characterized by the privatization of institutional learning
(Smith 1987).

Eye-to-eye contact

In a trenchant paper published in 1991, Peters drew attention to the significance of the Russian use of the term *Zaochny* for distance education:

> *Zaochny* is the Russian word for 'distance' in distance education. It is remarkable as it means – etymologically speaking – 'without eye contact'. This implies that the decisive criterion according to which distance education can be distinguished from conventional teaching and learning is the lack of eye contact. Distance education does not take place 'eyeball to eyeball' as Wedemeyer once called it. As the eye is the organ of man's innermost feelings, this aspect of apartness is surely significant. We become aware that a whole dimension of the interaction of the teacher and learner is lacking in distance education. The new form of teaching and learning is defined and characterized by pointing to a severe deficiency.
>
> (Peters 1991: 52)

This analysis draws attention to the provision of face-to-face contact in distance systems. Some systems had promoted no contact, claiming that students enrolled with them because they did not want to travel to college; some provided voluntary seminars to which the students who needed them could travel, leaving others the option of studying on their own; some insisted on compulsory seminars or induction meetings or summer schools, claiming that the educational experience would be inadequate without them. Other systems provided electronic meetings: linking students by audioconferences, teleconferences or videoconferences.

At the same time as Peters' remarks on eye-to-eye contact came the first reports (Bramble and Martin 1995) of successful face-to-face teaching at a distance by compressed video codec linkages. Students could see and hear the teacher and all the other students in the system and be seen and heard by them, even though they were hundreds or thousands of kilometres away. Eye-to-eye contact has been (electronically) restored. This raises questions, as yet unresolved, of the advantages or disadvantages of electronic meetings, voluntary or compulsory, in addition to or in replacement of face-to-face meetings in distance education.

CONCLUSION

In the light of these considerations the following definition of distance education is proposed.

Distance education is a form of education characterized by:

- the quasi-permanent separation of teacher and learner throughout the length of the learning process (this distinguishes it from conventional face-to-face education);
- the influence of an educational organization both in the planning and preparation of learning materials and in the provision of student support services (this distinguishes it from private study and teach-yourself programmes);
- the use of technical media – print, audio, video or computer – to unite teacher and learner and carry the content of the course;
- the provision of two-way communication so that the student may benefit from or even initiate dialogue (this distinguishes it from other uses of technology in education); and
- the quasi-permanent absence of the learning group throughout the length of the learning process so that people are usually taught as individuals rather than in groups, with the possibility of occasional meetings, either face-to-face or by electronic means, for both didactic and socialization purposes.

The definition seeks to take up the middle ground between the extremes of defining distance education so narrowly that it becomes an abstraction which does not correspond to existing reality, or so broadly that it becomes meaningless as the basis for analysis and the development of grounded theory.

Comparative studies of distance systems show that the element of face-to-face contact may be either non-existent, compulsory, or voluntary. The volume of face-to-face contact that would be consistent with the definition adopted for this study is indicated by the phrase 'the quasi-permanent separation of the learner from the teacher and from the learning group throughout the length of the learning process'. The linking of virtual classrooms by satellite, full bandwidth, compressed video or microwave links enables much of the content of a course to be taught at a distance.

The goal of this chapter has been to provide an accurate definition of distance education but not of all possibilities of educating at a distance. The range of 'education at a distance' is too vast and comprises both distance education as defined here and a range of other resource-based teaching and learning strategies. If the confusion of the past is to be avoided and if the goal of this study is to be achieved (the identification of a discrete area of educational activity in such a way that it can provide a basis for other scholars to build a valid theoretical structure and guides to good practice), then to be excluded from the concept of distance education are:

- the use of printed, audio-based, video-based, or computer-based learning materials in classroom, lecture theatres, seminars, tutorial, and laboratory sessions for on-campus programmes;

- the use of printed, audio-based, video-based learning materials and computers in private study.

REFERENCES

Aristotle (323 BC) *Nichomachaen Ethics*, 1.1

Bååth, J. (1981) 'On the nature of distance education', *Distance Education* 2(2), 212–13.

Barker, B., Frisbie, A. and Patrick, K. (1989) 'Broadening the definition of distance education in the light of the new telecommunications technologies', *The American Journal of Distance Education*, 3(1), 20–9.

Bramble, W. and Martin, B. (1995) 'The Florida Teletraining Project: military training via two-way compressed video', *The American Journal of Distance Education* 9(1), 6–26.

Delling, R. (1966) 'Versuch der Grundlegung zu einer systematischen Theorie des Fernunterrichts', in L. Sroka (ed.) *Fernunterricht 1966, Festschrift zum 50 Geburtstag von Walter Schultz-Rahe*, Hamburg: Hamburger Fernlehrinstitut.

Dohmen, G. (1967) *Das Fernstudium. Ein neues pädagogisches Forschungs- und Arbeitsfeld*, Tübingen: DIFF.

Edström, L. *et al.* (1970) *Mass Education: Studies in Adult Education and Teaching by Correspondence in some Developing Countries*, Stockholm: Almqvist & Wiksell.

Garrison, D. and Shale, D. (1987) 'Mapping the boundaries of distance education: problems in defining the field', *The American Journal of Distance Education* 1(1), 4–13.

Holmberg, B. (1977) *Distance Education: A Survey and Bibliography*, London: Kogan Page.

Keegan, D. (1980) 'On defining distance education', *Distance Education* 1(1), 13–36.

Markowitz, H. (1983) 'Independent study by correspondence in American universities', *Distance Education* 4(2), 149–70.

Moore, M. (1973) 'Toward a theory of independent learning and teaching', *Journal of Higher Education* 44, 661–79.

Moore M. (1977) *On a Theory of Independent Study*, Hagen: Fernuniversität (ZIFF).

Moore, M. (1990) 'Background and overview of contemporary American distance education', in M. Moore (ed.) *Contemporary Issues in American Distance Education*, New York: Pergamon, pp. xii–xxvi.

Peters, O. (1965) *Der Fernunterricht*, Weinheim: Beltz.

Peters, O. (1968) *Das Hochschulfernstudium*, Weinheim: Beltz.

Peters, O. (1973) *Die didaktische Struktur des Fernunterrichts*, Weinheim: Beltz.

Peters, O. (1991) 'Towards a better understanding of distance education: analysing designations and catchwords', in B. Holmberg and G. Ortner (eds) *Research into Distance Education*, Frankfurt: Lang.

Portway P. and Lane C. (eds) (1994) *Guide to Teleconferencing and Distance Learning*, San Ramon Calif.: Applied Business Communications.

Rumble, G. (1986) *The Planning and Management of Distance Education*, London: Croom Helm.

Rumble, G. (1995) 'Labour market theories and distance education: how Fordist is distance education?, *Open Learning*, June, 12–20.

Scheffler, I. (1968) *The Philosophy of Education*, New York: Wiley.

Smith, P. (1987) 'Distance education and educational change', in P. Smith and M. Kelly (eds) *Distance Education and the Mainstream*, London: Croom Helm.

Sparkes, J. (1987) Book review, *Studies in Higher Education* 12(2), 237–8.

Wedemeyer, C. (1977) 'Independent study', in A. Knowles (ed.) *The International Encyclopedia of Higher Education*, Boston: Northeastern University.

Willén, B. (1981) *Distance Education at Swedish Universities*, Stockholm: Almqvist & Wiksell.

Part II

THEORIES OF DISTANCE EDUCATION

4

INDEPENDENCE AND AUTONOMY

> It is unfortunately true that the failure of correspondence
> study to develop a theory related to the mainstream of
> educational thought and practice has seriously handi-
> capped the development and recognition of this field.
>
> Charles A. Wedemeyer, 1974

INTRODUCTION

Early pioneers of correspondence education, William Rainey
Harper of Chicago, William H. Lightly of Wisconsin, and Hans
Hermod of Malmö, wrote with verve and enthusiasm about the
advantages of this form of education. But the historian of distance education, Rudolf Manfred Delling from Tübingen,
claimed in 1966 that although institutionalized distance education had existed for about a hundred years, it was only during
the previous few years that the practice of distance teaching had
commenced to rely on theory. Nevertheless there was no systematic theory of distance education which might make it possible to classify practitioners' individual experiences in relation
to their essence (1966: 183). Delling states that the first theoretical work was developed in the 1950s. In 1959 the East German scholar Joannes Riechert of Freiburg published a book
Schreiben, Lehren und Verstehen (Write, Teach and Learn), and
at about the same time from Sweden came an international
description of the field *On the Methods of Teaching by Correspondence* by Börje Holmberg (1960). This was translated into German in 1962.

When theoretical approaches began to emerge in the 1970s,

55

their development was fitful. The first major theoretical structure, and to date the most comprehensive (Peters 1973), categorized distance education as an industrialization of the education process and suggested that the closest parallel to a distance-teaching organization was the industrialized production of goods. A mail order firm would have a structure similar to an institution for this form of education.

The claim of Wedemeyer that distance education has failed 'to develop a theory related to the mainstream of educational thought and practice' remains true today. The following chapters attempt a detailed analysis of the theoretical approaches that have been attempted to date. They are presented here because they are among the best available in the literature and because it is correct to present a detailed exposé of the work of previous writers before attempting to suggest a new basis for theoretical structure. Nascent, if fragile, theoretical proposals have been found in the writings of Moore, Peters, and Holmberg; ideas of value have been contributed by Delling, Wedemeyer, Bååth, Daniel, Smith, and Sewart.

For the purposes of this book the more important positions formulated to date are classified into three groupings:

- *Theories of autonomy and independence.* These contributions come mainly from the late 1960s and early 1970s and the major representatives are Rudolf Manfred Delling (Germany), Charles A. Wedemeyer (USA) and Michael G. Moore (USA) (chapter 4).
- *Theory of industrialization.* Otto Peters' work in Germany comprised comparative studies throughout the 1960s and theoretical formulation in the early 1970s (chapter 5).
- *Theories of interaction and communication.* More contemporary views from Börje Holmberg (Sweden/Germany), John A. Bååth (Sweden), David Sewart (UK), Kevin C. Smith (Australia), and John S. Daniel (Canada/UK) (chapter 6).

In 1993 Amundsen published a major analysis of the evolution of theoretical writing on distance education, adding presentation of the work of D.R. Garrison (Canada) and J. Verduin and T. Clark (United States) to the authors presented here (Amundsen 1993: 61–79).

A HELPING ORGANIZATION

Rudolf Manfred Delling of the Deutsches Institut für Fernstudienforschung an der Universität Tübingen is a historian and bibliographer. In 1966 he provided this definition:

> Distance education (*Fernunterricht*) is a planned and systematic activity which comprises the choice, didactic preparation and presentation of teaching materials as well as the supervision and support of student learning and which is achieved by bridging the physical distance between student and teacher by means of at least one appropriate technical medium.
>
> (Delling 1966: 186)

Delling sees distance education as a multi-dimensional system of learning and communication processes, with the aid of an artificial signal-carrier. In many of his writings (1968, 1978) he lists eight dimensions:

- a learner;
- society (including legislation, administration, family, etc.);
- a helping organization (distance teaching institutions);
- a learning objective;
- the content to be learned;
- the result of learning;
- distance;
- a signal-carrier.

Remarkable in his approach are his hesitation to label distance education a teaching process (distance colleges or departments are organizations which 'help' learning) and the absence of the teacher from the eight dimensions of the system.

A distance education course is an artificial, dialogic opportunity for learning in which the distance between the learner and the helping organization is bridged by an artificial signal-carrier.

From the start the concepts of feedback and two-way communications are central to Delling's position. He sees an essential difference between learning opportunities that are *monologues* (books, newspapers, journals, documentary films, lectures without discussion, broadcasts, self-teaching courses, and other self-instructional material) and those that are *dialogic* (normal classroom or school teaching, conversations, letters with answers, and distance education courses). Monologues are based on one-way communication, whereas dialogues are characterized by two-way communication.

The world of distance education, he claims, has little of the characteristics of 'teaching' because there is, in general, no teacher in the system and the functions relating to student learning within the helping organization are performed by a variety of machines, people, and materials.

Delling tends to reduce the role of the teacher and of the educational organization to a minimum and throw the whole emphasis on the autonomy and independence of the learner. This is especially important because adults are normally the learners in distance programmes. Adults do not, he suggests, accept the conventional educator-pupil relationship. The function of the 'helping organization' is to take over, upon the wish of learners, everything that they cannot yet do for themselves, with the tendency that the learners eventually become autonomous. When this occurs the only function left for the helping organization is to provide information, documentation, and library facilities.

Delling seems to want to place distance education outside the field of educational theory. He sees it falling within the range of communication processes and to be characterized by industrialized mechanisms which carry on its artificial dialogic and two-way communication processes. He reduces to a minimum the role of the teacher and throw the whole weight of his analysis on the learning of the student studying at a distance.

In 1994 Delling published a major analysis of open and distance learning terminology from his work at the Deutsches Institut für Fernstudienforschung (German Institute for Distance Education Research) at Tübingen.

INDEPENDENT STUDY

The term 'independent study' was used by Charles A. Wedemeyer to describe distance education at university level. For much of his professional life he was Professor of Education at the University of Wisconsin, Madison and closely associated with the Independent Study Division of the National University Extension Association of the United States of America.

He uses the term 'independent study' to describe distance education at university level and gives this definition:

> 'Independent learning' is that learning, that changed behaviour, that results from activities carried on by learners in space and time, learners whose environment is different from that of the school, learners who may be guided by teachers but who are not dependent upon them, learners who accept degrees of freedom and responsibility in initiating and carrying out the activities that lead to learning.
>
> (Wedemeyer 1973: 73)

Wedemeyer's thought is generous and liberal. A major influence is the philosophy of Carl Rogers. There are two bases for his views on independent study: a democratic social ideal and a liberal educational philosophy. He considers that nobody should be denied the opportunity to learn because he/she is poor, geographically isolated, socially disadvantaged, in poor health, institutionalized, or otherwise unable to place himself/herself within the institution's special environment for learning. Thus he claims that independent study should be self-pacing, individualized, and offer freedom in goal selection.

The independent learner

Wedemeyer sees the independent learner as the original or 'proto'-learner whose success in learning enables him/her to survive and he claims that each individual commences with a period of pre-school individual learning. Group instruction which evolved in schools was first intended, he tells us, for the elite, and the long history of formal education is characterized by a persistent pattern of the learner in the group – a *dependent* learner whose goals, activities, rewards, and punishments are decided by the policies and practices of an ever-present group of teachers.

The pattern of the learner in the group underwent a gradual breakdown process in which he sees the space and time barriers to independent study being dissipated in six successive stages:

1 The invention of writing.
2 The invention of printing.
3 The invention of correspondence education: the first formally

structured format for the independent learner, which made use of new technology in the form of a reliable mail service in the mid-1800s.

4 Development of democratic and egalitarian philosophies.
5 Application of telecommunications media to teaching.
6 Development of programmed-learning theory.

(Wedemeyer 1973: 75)

These series of developments led in his own day to the possibility for people, cut off from the regular schools, to continue learning in ever larger numbers. Wedemeyer uses three terms for such programmes: 'independent study', 'open learning', and 'distance education'. He saw in the 1960s the re-emergence of the independent learner, with a new elan for independent programmes in areas where conventional group-based formal learning was less able to succeed.

'Independent study'

Wedemeyer made a determined effort to establish the term 'independent study' as the umbrella term for this field of education both in the US and throughout the world:

> Independent study consists of various forms of teaching–learning arrangements in which teachers and learners carry out their essential tasks and responsibilities apart from one another, communicating in a variety of ways. Its purposes are to free on-campus or internal learners from inappropriate class placings or patterns, to provide off-campus or external learners with the opportunity to continue learning in their own environments, and developing in all learners the capacity to carry on self-directed learning, the ultimate maturity required of the educated person.
>
> (Wedemeyer 1977: 2114)

It will be noticed at once that Wedemeyer's concept of 'independent study' comprises two different forms of education: 'independent study for the internal student' and 'independent study for the external student'. Independent study for the internal student makes freedom from lecture attendance possible for exceptional university students by the allocation of series of readings and individual study programmes. One can see elements in his thought of ideas similar to the contract programmes and educational brokerage ideas favoured in some experimental American programmes of the mid-1970s. The linking of external and internal programmes in the one definition, however, tends to diffuse Wedemeyer's ideas and the emphasis on internal independent study disappears in his later articles.

Wedemeyer's liberal educational theory and egalitarian social philosophy were ill-at-ease with the conventional educational system and many of his writings are marked by comments on the shortcomings of the contemporary scene both at school and university level:

> Conventional teaching and learning, makes use of concepts of learning and teaching that have preserved the old mystiques, that have maintained space–time barriers to learning.
> (Childs and Wedemeyer 1961: 71)

Within this context he set out a conceptual structure for an educational system that would be more akin to his views. Most of his writings list ten characteristics of the proposed system:

1 The system should be capable of operation any place where there are students – or even only one student – whether or not there are teachers at the same place at the same time.

2 The system should place greater responsibility for learning on the student.

3 The system should free faculty members from custodial type duties so that more time can be given to truly educational tasks.

4 The system should offer students and adults wider choices (more opportunities) in courses, formats, methodologies.

5 The system should use, as appropriate, all the teaching media and methods that have been proved effective.

6 The system should mix and combine media and methods so that each subject or unit within a subject is taught in the best way known.

7 The system should cause the redesign and development of courses to fit into an 'articulated media programme'.

8 The system should preserve and enhance opportunities for adaptation to individual differences.

9 The system should evaluate student achievement simply, not by raising barriers concerned *with the place* the student studies, the *rate* at which he studies, the *method* by which he studies or the *sequence* within which he studies.

10 The system should permit students to start, stop and learn at their own pace.

(Wedemeyer 1968: 328, 1981: 36)

Wedemeyer saw instinctively that the only way to break what he called the 'space–time barriers' of education was by separating teaching from learning. This involved planning each as a separate activity. These early insights by Wedemeyer were later confirmed by Kaye and Rumble (1987).

Planning teaching and learning as separate activities leads Wedemeyer to postulate six characteristics of distance or independent systems that are capable of operation any place there are students – or even only one student – whether or not there are teachers at the same place at the same time:

1 The student and teacher are separated.
2 The normal processes of teaching and learning are carried on in writing or through some other medium.
3 Teaching is individualized.
4 Learning takes place through the student's activity.
5 Learning is made convenient for the student in his own environment.
6 The learner takes responsibility for his progress, with freedom to start and stop at any time and to pace himself.

(Wedemeyer 1973: 76)

The teaching–learning situation

In many of his writings Wedemeyer presents his thoughts diagramatically. He claims that every teaching–learning situation comprises four elements:

- a teacher;
- a learner or learners;

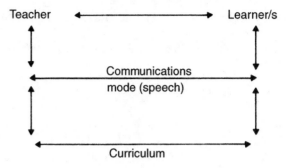

Figure 4.1 The classroom as a teaching–learning situation (Wedemeyer)
Source: Adapted from Keegan (1976)

- a communications system or mode;
- something to be taught/learned.

He then claims that a traditional classroom could be represented as a box which encompasses the four elements as shown in Figure 4.1.

In a number of his writings Wedemeyer explains what he has called the 'classroom-box':

> If the communications system is a given, either because it is the only system available (think of Plato meeting learners in the Grove of Akademos) or is a cultural artifact acting as an imperative, then there are no options, and the communication must be face-to-face, eyeball-to-eyeball, earpan-to-earpan speech. Then, if a box is put around the four essential elements, we have a classroom. A teaching–learning system that must work any place, any time, for one learner or many, directly confronts the space–time–elite barriers of the classroom model. In fact, however, distance has long been a problem in the classroom model. As classes became larger, and lectures replaced the dialogue that Plato conducted, the integrity of the model was breached. Only the illusion of being effectively face-to-face remains, as distance within the box lengthens between teacher and learners and speech is amplified for ever more distant reception. The concept of 'distance' involves more than physical distance. There is social distance, cultural distance, and what I have been calling 'physical' distance for want of a better term. All of

these are present wherever teaching and learning are carried on.

(Wedemeyer 1978: 13–14, 1981: 38–40)

However, if we are to achieve a 'teaching–learning system that must work any place, any time, for one learner or many', Wedemeyer tells us that the 'classroom-box' (Figure 4.1) must be restructured as in Figure 4.2 where the four elements of the previous structure remain but have been reorganized to accommodate physical space. This representation of the teaching–learning process by Wedemeyer to accommodate the 'any time, any place, single or multiple learner's requirements' has as its aim the organization of instruction so that greater freedom in learning is possible. As an outcome of this he proposes three conceptualizations of freedom for learners in all independent or distance programmes:

- learning should be self-pacing: the learner should be able to pace his studies in accordance with his circumstances and needs
- learning should be individualized and the learners should be free to follow any of several courses of learning
- the learner should have freedom in selection of goals and activities.

(Wedemeyer 1973: 101)

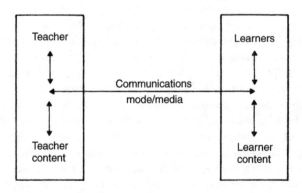

Figure 4.2 A teaching–learning situation to accommodate physical distance (Wedemeyer)
Source: Adapted from Keegan (1976)

Structuring the system

Wedemeyer ran into some criticism when he tried to suggest that these theoretical propositions about the freedom of the distance learner should be implemented in practice. These criticisms came both from those looking for a workable system and from those who feared that public monies spent on distance systems would be transferred back to conventional education if the learning in the distance system could not be accurately evaluated or if the evaluation was that the learning in the independent system was inferior.

Despite the idealistic nature of much of Wedemeyer's writing he had a very extensive knowledge of the day-to-day workings of correspondence systems. 'Not every student', he warns, 'will be able to succeed by correspondence instruction. This is *not* an easy method of learning' (1963: 30).

He details five serious obstacles to success as a distance learner:

- developing interest in the task and motivation
- readiness for study is a problem in correspondence study witnessed by 'the non-start, the early drop-out, the under achiever'
- grasping the structure of the subject to be learned at a distance
- learning both analytic and instructive thinking
- evaluating progress in learning.

(Wedemeyer 1962: 14)

The secret of success in Wedemeyer's thought is placed squarely on the shoulders of the instructor who is in a continuous tutorial relationship with the correspondence student. The teacher is the daily monitor and motivator of the distance student. The chief value of the correspondence method lies in the tutorial relationship developed between the teacher and the student, and to minimize or destroy this relationship (by check-off type lessons, multiple-choice answers) actually changes the character of the work offered. Schools that depend solely on the use of objective or machine-type scoring have abandoned distance education. Such programmes are, in fact, programmes of 'self-study' (1963: 29).

In a similar vein Wedemeyer does not consider close-circuit

television, radio, telephone, teaching machines, computer, and satellite as forms of independent study or distance education except under strict conditions: 'If media (CCTV, for example) are employed merely to replicate a regular class without broadening opportunity and shifting responsibility and freedom to the learner, the system cannot be defined as independent study' (1971: 552).

Evaluation

Wedemeyer undertook the uphill struggle of trying to promote non-traditional education programmes in the highly structured US university scene. The rather bleak title he chose for the edited collection of his writings published on his retirement, *Learning at the Back-Door* (1981), shows his own assessment of the Sisyphan task of gaining status for non-traditional, open, and distance programmes for credit in the US.

His earlier writings are more incisive than his later articles which tend to reproduce with precision ideas presented earlier. All the important ideas are there in the 1960s and there is little reformulation in the 1970s. Although the writings of the 1960s show familiarity with the day-to-day problems of the organization of independent programmes and the difficulties of both teaching and learning at a distance, he does not deal with planning mechanisms or management analyses that would allow others to build on his ideas.

Wedemeyer's personal dedication, generosity, and liberal vision contributed much to the growth of a consensus among distance educators throughout the world and influenced many of the writers treated in the next chapters.

AUTONOMY AND DISTANCE

Writing in 1973, Michael G. Moore, formerly of the University of Wisconsin at Madison, then of the Open University of the United Kingdom and today at Pennsylvania State University, complained that progress in distance education was being hindered by lack of attention to what he called the 'macro-factors':

- description;
- definition;

- discrimination;
- identification;
- building a theoretical framework.

His own contribution was the development of a theory of distance education based on the variables 'autonomy' and 'distance'.

Moore's first contributions to a theory of distance education came in the early 1970s but they read with surprising freshness today. A number of themes are immediately apparent in his writing: he states clearly that he wishes to develop a theory of education at a distance, defines which aspects of educational endeavour he is dealing with and which are excluded, speaks of those students who will not attend groupings but choose to learn apart from teachers, uses confidently terms like 'distance teaching' and 'distance education' as 'a field of education' at a time when most were classifying it merely as a method or a mode (Moore 1975).

Moore's focus is on all forms of deliberate, planned, structured learning and teaching that are carried on outside the school environment. He defines the school environment as 'the classroom, lecture or seminar, the setting in which the events of teaching are contemporaneous and co-terminous with the events of learning'. Distance education (he uses the term 'independent learning and teaching') is an educational system in which the learner is autonomous and separated from the teacher by space and time so that communication is by a non-human medium. The distance system has three subsystems: a learner, a teacher and a method of communication. These subsystems have critical characteristics distinguishing them from learning, teaching, and communication in other forms of education.

His research began with the belief that instruction can be considered as comprising two families of teaching activities: face-to-face or 'contiguous' teaching and 'distance teaching'. From an exhaustive search of the literature, Moore lists the forms of educational provision that fall within his concept of 'distance teaching': an open university, a university without walls, an independent study programme on-campus, an external degree programme, and even a teach-yourself book. This is a much wider classification than that accepted for distance education in this book. The reason for it is, as with Wedemeyer, the inclusion of on-campus independent study programmes within the definition, and an opening up of the concept 'independence' to include programmes without two-way communication.

Within this theoretical structure Moore identifies two clusters of educational offerings as essential components of independent study:

- programmes designed for learners in environments apart from their instructors – distance teaching: and
- programmes designed for the encouragement of independent/self-directed learning – learner autonomy.

Here he brings together two traditions: distance teaching which he traces back (with Noffsinger) to the 1840s and self-directed study which he traces back through a range of practices in American higher education to the tutor system in Oxford University in the nineteenth century.

Distance teaching is defined as the family of instructional methods in which the teaching behaviours are executed apart from the learning behaviours, including those behaviours that in a contiguous situation would be performed in the learner's presence, so that communication between the teacher and the learner must be facilitated by print, electronic, mechanical, or other devices (1977a).

Moore accepted that teaching consists of two phases: 'the preactive' and the 'interactive'. For Moore, the teacher in the preactive phase selects objectives and plans the curriculum and instructional strategies. In the 'interactive' phase, face to face with learners, the teacher provides verbal stimulation, makes explanations, asks questions, and provides guidance (1977b: 15).

He is clearly concerned that most educational research treats teaching as 'the activity which takes place *during* school and *within* the classroom setting' where communication is by the human voice and there is 'immediate, spontaneous, often emotionally-motivated interaction between the learner and the teacher, and usually between the learner and other learners: there is a social interactional relationship which assumes no delay in communication, no distance in space or time'. Since the introduction of compulsory education for children, Moore points out, face-to-face teaching has been accepted as the norm. But distance teaching situations do exist, particularly with adult learners.

The concept of distance

Moore correctly identifies the concept of separation of learner and teacher as the origin of the concept 'distance' in education, and as crucial for determining the selection of research data from which theoretical frameworks in this field may be constructed. Basic to Moore's position is that distance teaching programmes can be classified according to the distance between learner and teacher. He wants programmes to be classified by the provision for two-way communication (dialogue or D) and by the extent to which a programme can be responsive to a learner's individual needs (structure or S). He believes that the element of two-way communication in all distance teaching programmes can be measured and suggests that an educational telephone network is an example of high two-way communication or dialogue (+D) and an educational radio broadcast is an example of a distance teaching methodology in which two-way communication is *not* possible (− D) and hence would not be counted as an example of distance education as defined in this book. (He is classifying educational uses of media, not communications media.)

Moore also measures programmes in so far as they are responsive to students' needs as individuals, and labels this 'structure'.

Table 4.1 Types of distance teaching programmes (Moore)

	Type	Programme Types	Examples
Most distance	−D−S	1 Programmes with no dialogue and no structure	Independent reading–study programmes of the 'self-directed' kind
	−D+S	2 Programmes with no dialogue but with structure	Programmes in which the communication method is radio or television
	+D+S	3 Programmes with dialogue and structure	Typically, programmes using the correspondence method
Least distance	+D−S	4 Programmes with dialogue and no structure	A Rogerian type of tutorial programme

Source: Adapted from Moore (1977a)

In a highly structured programme (+S) no variation of the programme is possible (as in a Linear Programmed Instruction Text), but when there is a minimum of structure teachers and learners can respond easily to stimuli. Thus Moore feels it is important to measure the extent of the responsiveness of a teaching programme to a learner's individual needs, goals, progress, or achievements (is it highly structured or not?) whether the communications medium on which it is based permits two-way communication or not. He presents this as in Table 4.1 (with S representing structure and D dialogue).

The concept of autonomy

The more tentative section of Moore's theory is when he tries to establish learner autonomy as the second dimension of independent learning (1972).

In his various publications Moore writes well on the autonomy of the independent learner. There is a strong humanistic tendency in his writing. He is influenced by Charles Wedemeyer, Carl Rogers, Allan Tough, and Malcolm Knowles, but the synthesis is his own. Starting from a general observation that learners both in schools and universities are very dependent on teachers for explanations, guidance, questions, and stimulation, Moore shows that such an approach places more decision-making powers in the hands of the teacher than is acceptable to some adult education theorists.

Like Wedemeyer he seeks for learner autonomy in:

- the setting of objectives;
- methods of study;
- evaluation.

There *are* possible programmes, he tells us, that achieve these goals but most do not. Both in conventional education and in most programmes of distance teaching and learning, Moore supports Maslow's analysis that the teacher is the active one who teaches a passive person. This person is shaped and taught and is given something which he or she then accumulates and which they may lose or retain. This kind of learning, he tells us, too easily reflects the goals of the teacher, and ignores the values and ends of the learner (1977b: 21).

The basis for learner autonomy as a necessary theoretical

component of distance education is justified by Moore from his analysis of the separation between teacher and learner in education at a distance. He asks whether the concept of 'distance' or 'separation' or 'apartness' is adequate to explain the gap between teacher and learner. His own answer is no. The existence of this gap means that the activities of teachers and learners will be influenced by it. Because the learner *is* alone, he is compelled to accept a comparatively high degree of responsibility for the conduct of the learning programme. The learner also exercises a greater degree of control over his/her learning.

The autonomous learner proceeds without need for admonition and little need for direction. If highly autonomous he/she may have no personal relationship with a teacher but if he/she *has* a personal teacher he/she will be able to control the effect and significance of teacher input in a realistic and unemotional way. To the highly autonomous learner the teacher's role is that of respondent rather than director and the institution becomes a helping organization.

There are some adult learners who need help in formulating their learning objectives and in identifying sources of information and in measuring achievements, whereas there are many others who are autonomous learners, with the abilities of self-stimulation, knowledge of ways to achieve their objectives, and ways of measuring achievement. It is necessary, therefore, to be able to measure the 'autonomy' dimension of educational programmes. Moore sets out to do this in terms of his statement that all teaching–learning processes have these characteristic components:

- *establishment or preparatory activities* in which problems are identified, goals set and strategies planned
- *executive activities* in which data, information and ideas are patterned, experiments and tests take place in order to arrive at instructional solutions
- *evaluatory activities* in which the instructional processes make judgements about the appropriateness of the information and ideas for solving the problems and meeting the goals.

(Moore 1977b: 21)

Moore claims that in conventional education the establishment activities are entirely in the purview of the teacher, whereas at a distance the teacher merely prepares instructional materials to be used and drawn upon to the extent that the learner desires. The teacher hopes that his/her material will meet the goals established by learners and will be used in their executive activities. In distance education, whether or not the material is used remains outside the distant teacher's control, and is dependent almost entirely on the worth of the material, as distant learners accept only executive material that meets their goals.

Similarly in evaluation, the conventional teacher invariably establishes both the criteria of successful learning and passes judgement on whether the criteria are satisfied. Where the teachers' and learners' goals do not coincide the latter invariably compromise through fear, apathy, or courtesy. Learner autonomy is heightened by distance and the learner is compelled by distance to assume a degree of autonomy that might be uncomfortable in other circumstances.

Classification of programmes

Programmes are classified according to the extent to which the learner can exercise autonomy in learning by asking three questions:

- *Autonomy in setting of objectives?* Is the selection of learning objectives in the programme that of the learner or the teacher?
- *Autonomy in methods of study?* Is the selection and use of resource persons, of bodies, and other media, the decision of the teacher or the learner?
- *Autonomy in evaluation?* Are the decisions about the method of evaluation and criteria to be used made by the learner or the teacher?

By applying these questions to teaching programmes Moore arrives at the classification shown in Table 4.2 in which A = learner determined (autonomous) and N = teacher determined (non-autonomous). An indication of the type of programme Moore might be considering is given for each of his eight categories.

Since learner autonomy is the extent to which in an independent study programme the learner determines the objectives,

Table 4.2 Types of independent study programmes by variable of learner autonomy (Moore)

Example	Objective setting	Implemen- tation	Evaluation
1 Private study	A	A	A
2 University of London External Degree	A	A	N
3 Learning sports skills	A	N	A
4 Learning car driving	A	N	N
5 Learner controls course and evaluation	N	A	A
6 Learner controls evaluation	N	N	A
7 Many independent study courses	N	A	N
8 Independent study for credit	N	N	N

A = Learner determined ('autonomous').
N = Teacher determined ('non-autonomous')
Source: Adapted from Moore (1977a)

implementation strategies and evaluation, and since distance means a combination of the availability of two-way communication plus the extent to which a programme is adaptable to the individuality of students, it follows that Moore can classify all educational programmes by his own variables 'distance' and 'autonomy'. This he proposes to do by superimposing Table 4.1 on Table 4.2 in such a way that he can categorize all educational programmes so that they range from having most independent to the least independent study.

In Figure 4.3 type AAA−D−S represents the most independent form of education: totally private study with no two-way communication and completely unstructured with the learner entirely autonomous in goals, methods, and evaluation. Type NNN+D−S is the least independent, where autonomy and distance are very low and the learner is completely controlled by the teacher.

Thus, for Moore, independent study is any educational programme in which the learning programme occurs separate in time and place from the teaching programme, and in which the learner has an influence equal to the teacher's in determining learning goals, resources, and evaluation decisions.

Figure 4.3 Typology of educational programmes (Moore)
Source: Adapted from Moore (1977a)

But learners vary in the extent to which they are able to exercise autonomy and hence there is no value judgement in the use of the terms 'autonomy' and 'distance'. There are programmes with much autonomy and dialogue and programmes with less, and they vary in distance. A programme of high autonomy may be as damaging to a person as one of low autonomy. The problem is to match programmes to learners so that each learner exercises the maximum autonomy and grows.

Evaluation

The first pole of his theoretical position 'distance' is well established, but further contribution is required from Moore to justify 'autonomy' (1972, 1983) as a second pole.

Moore published a reappraisal of his position in 1993 under the title 'Theory of transactional distance'. In this study he adapts his views analysed above to the introduction of electronic telecommunications media into the field:

Since the theory of Transactional Distance was written, the most important evolution in distance education has been the development of highly interactive telecommunications media. This is the family of teleconference media – i.e., the use of interactive computer networks and audio, audio-graphic, and video networks, which may be local, regional, national and international and are linked by cable, microwave and satellite. The use has added the possibility of faster dialogue with the teacher and, by computerconferencing, more individual dialogue. These media provide less structured programmes than the recorded or print-media. Above all, the teleconference media allow a new form of dialogue that can be called inter-learner dialogue. Inter-learner dialogue occurs between learners and other learners, alone or in groups, with or without the real-time presence of an instructor. By audioconference, videoconference, and computer conference, groups can learn through interaction with other groups and within groups.

(Moore 1993: 32)

At the time of writing Moore is academic director of the American Center for the Study of Distance Education at Pennsylvania State University.

REFERENCES

Amundsen, C. (1993) 'The evolution of theory in distance education', pp. 61–79 in D. Keegan (ed.) *Theoretical Principles of Distance Education*, London: Routledge.

Childs, G. and Wedemeyer, C.A. (1961) *New Perspectives in University Correspondence Study*, Chicago: Center for Study of Education of Adults.

Delling, R.M. (1966) 'Versuch der Grundlegung zu einer systematischen Theorie des Fernunterrichts', in L. Sroka (ed.) *Fernunterrricht 1966, Festschrift zum 50 Geburtstag von Walter Schultz-Rahe*, Hamburg: Hamburger Fernlehrinstitut.

Delling, R.M. (1968) 'Protokoll des I Brief-Symposions über Fernunterrich und Fernstudium', *Epistolodidaktika* 1 (Sonderheft), 6–10.

Delling, R.M. (1978) 'Briefwechsel als Bestandteil und Vorlaufer des Fernstudiums' (*Ziff Papiere 19*), Hagen: Fernuniversität (ZIFF).

Delling, R.M. (1994) 'Offenes Lernen – ein Literaturbericht', pp. 191–226 in G. Zimmer (ed.) *Vom Fernunterricht zum Open Distance Learning; eine europäische Initiative*, Berlin: BIBB.

Holmberg, B. (1960) *On the Methods of Teaching by Correspondenc*, Lund: Gleerup.

Kaye, A. and Rumble, G. (1978) *Distance Teaching for Higher and Adult Education*, London: Croom Helm.

Keegan, D. (ed.) (1976) *TAFE Distance Education in South Australia*, Adelaide: Open College.

Moore, M. (1972) 'Learner autonomy: the second dimension of independent learning', *Convergence* 5(2), 76–8.

Moore, M. (1973) 'Toward a theory of independent learning and teaching', *Journal of Higher Education* 44, 661–79.

Moore, M. (1975) 'Cognitive style and telemathic (distance) teaching', *ICCE Newsletter* 4, 3–10.

Moore, M. (1977a) 'A model of independent study', *Epistolodidaktika* 1, 6–40.

Moore, M. (1977b) *On a Theory of Independent Study*, Hagen: Fernuniversität.

Moore, M. (1983) 'The individual adult learner', in M. Tight (ed.) *Adult Learning and Education*, London: Croom Helm.

Moore, M. (1993) 'Theory of transactional distance', pp. 22–38 in D. Keegan (ed.) *Theoretical Principles of Distance Education*, London: Routledge.

Peters, O. (1973) *Die didaktische Struktur des Fernunterrichts*, Weinheim: Beltz.

Reichert, J. (1959) *Schreiben, Lehren und Verstehen*, Freiburg: Bergakademie.

Wedemeyer, C. (1962) *Report of the Conference on Newer Media in Correspondence Study*, Austin, Tex.: University of Texas, pp. 10–14.

Wedemeyer, C. (1963) 'Going to college at home', *Home Study Review* 4(3), 24–32.

Wedemeyer, C. (1968) 'With whom will you dance? The new educational technology', *Journal of the American Dietetic Association* 53, 325–8.

Wedemeyer, C. (1971) 'Independent study', pp. 548–57 in L. Deighton (ed.) *The Encyclopedia of Education*, Vol. 4, New York: Macmillan.

Wedemeyer, C. (1973) 'The use of correspondence education for post-secretary education', in A. Kabwasa and M. Kaunda (eds) *Correspondence Education in Africa*, London: Routledge & Kegan Paul.

Wedemeyer, C. (1974) 'Characteristics of open learning systems', in *Open Learning Systems*, Washington: National Association of Educational Broadcasters.

Wedemeyer, C. (1977) 'Independent study', pp. 2114–32 in A.S. Knowles (ed.) *The International Encyclopedia of Higher Education*, Boston: CIHED.

Wedemeyer, C. (1978) 'Criteria for constructing and distance education system', *Canadian Journal of University of Continuing Education* 6(1), 9–15.

Wedemeyer, C. (1981) *Learning at the Back-Door*, Madison: University of Wisconsin.

5

THE INDUSTRIALIZATION OF TEACHING

Anyone professionally involved in education is obliged to presume the existence of two forms of instruction which are strictly separable: traditional face-to-face teaching based on interpersonal communication and industrialized teaching which is based on an objectivized, rationalized, technologically-produced interaction.

O. Peters, 1973

INTRODUCTION

Much of the early research work in distance education was accomplished by Otto Peters in the early 1960s. Peters worked at the German Institute for Distance Education (DIFF) at Tübingen in the Federal Republic of Germany, then at the Berlin College of Education before becoming in 1975 the foundation Vice-Chancellor (*Gründungsrektor*) of the Fernuniversität in Hagen. In 1965 he published an authoritative analytical and comparative survey of distance institutions at further educational level throughout the world. This was followed in 1968 by a survey of distance teaching at higher education level.

Peters states that when his analytical and comparative analysis of distance teaching systems was complete, he proceeded to develop a theoretical structure for the field. He claims that the traditional categories of educational research proved inadequate for a didactical analysis of distance systems and he was forced to abandon them. Building up systems for teaching at a distance, he tells us, is structured so differently from conventional, oral

77

education that the didactical analyst must look elsewhere for his models.

For Peters the most fruitful model was the similarities between the industrial production process and the teaching–learning process in distance education. He analysed the industrial production process and found that not only did this provide a satisfactory basis for an analysis of distance teaching but that a fruitful explanatory and forecasting theory of teaching at a distance was possible when one considered it as the most industrialized form of teaching and learning.

Peters justified his search for a new theoretical basis for distance teaching on the grounds that it is a new form of industrialized and technological education. He states that from many points of view conventional, oral, group-based education is a pre-industrial form of education. In the universities of the Middle Ages, the ancient rhetorical form of education was replaced by the lecture, the seminar, and the lesson and these have remained permanent characteristics of traditional education ever since. The humanistic influence added the tutorial. These can all be regarded as pre-industrialized forms of education in which the individual lecturer remains in close contact with the whole teaching process just as an artisan does with his craft. Attempts to adapt the lecture, seminar, and tutorial to industrialized techniques by the use of educational technology will not prove successful because of the pre-industrial characteristics of the didactic structures in conventional universities.

Distance teaching, however, is recent. It could not have existed before the industrial era. It began, at most, 130 years ago, he says, writing in 1980. It was no historical accident that correspondence education and the industrialization of society began about the same time because they are intrinsically linked. Distance education is impossible without a relatively fast and regular postal service and transport system: 'the first railway lines and the first correspondence schools were established around the same time'.

Traditional educational concepts are only of partial use in analysing and describing this industrialized form of education so new categories for analysis must be found and they can best be found from the sciences which analyse industrial processes.

All forms of human life have been heavily influenced by the Industrial Revolution. Only traditional forms of education in schools, colleges, and universities have remained outside it – except for the phenomenon of education at a distance.

Peters claims some basis for his comparative study from the fact that the production of learning materials for distance students is, in itself, an industrialized process and one that is, in its didactic procedures, quite different from book production.

DIDACTICAL ANALYSIS

Peters' theoretical presentation of distance teaching commences with a didactical analysis. In this presentation distance teaching is analysed as a distinct field of educational endeavour and not as a teaching 'mode'. The analysis of the didactic structure of distance teaching (1976: 3–17) follows exactly the structures proposed by Paul Heimann and Wolfgang Schultz, two German educational theorists who founded the Berlin School of Didactics – now also referred to as the Hamburg model, as Schultz became a professor at the University of Hamburg (Heidt 1978: 48; Holmberg 1982: 139).

Heimann and Schultz claim that all teaching–learning processes can be analysed in terms of six intrinsic structural elements: aims, content, methods, choice of medium, human prerequisites, and socio-cultural prerequisites. Peters analyses distance education, as Heimann and Schultz had analysed education in general, in terms of these six essential structures of the educational process and has little difficulty in demonstrating profound structural differences between distance education and conventional education for all six of the constituent characteristics (1967: 4–16).

- *Aim*: The aim of distance teaching is determined by structural considerations as in all forms of teaching. Specific structural differences in the cognitive, emotional, and practical domains are indicated for distance teaching.
- *Contents*: The teaching of knowledge, skills, and practical 'hand-on' learning are examined and the difficulties and/or possibility of teaching certain content at a distance is considered.
- *Methods*: The drastic reduction or complete suppression of interpersonal communication is treated and its substitution by written information carriers and motivators.

- *Choice of medium*: It is claimed that communication suffers an essential loss of substance in its transfer from human speech to the written word and the possible compensating role of other media is considered.
- *Human prerequisites*: Employment conditions, age, diagnostic counselling for entry to courses are contrasted with the condition of conventional students.
- *Socio-cultural prerequisites*: Ideological, political, academic status, and tradition aspects of distance education in different cultures (USA, USSR, South Africa, England, Sweden) are considered.

The conclusion for Peters is inescapable. Distance education and conventional education have been shown to be essentially diverse on each of the six constituent components of an educational process as defined by the most 'adequate theoretical basis for dealing with instructional media' (Heidt 1978: 47) known to German educational theorists.

This analysis leads to a fundamental separation between direct and indirect teaching and the claim that educational theorists have focused on direct teaching, especially in its conventional, oral, group-based form, to the virtual exclusion of that other component of the educational scene – indirect teaching – of which distance teaching is one of the elements.

He lists the other components of teaching which are not direct, but which are not, however, to be identified as distance education: education by letter; printed learning materials; audio-visual teaching; educational radio and television; programmed learning; computer-based instruction; independent study; private study; and learning from teaching materials.

INDUSTRIAL COMPARISON

At this point in his treatment of the subject (1967, 1971, 1973) Peters presents a comparison of distance teaching and the industrial production of goods under the following headings: rationalization; division of labour; mechanization; assembly line; mass production; preparatory work; formalization; standardization; functional change; objectification; concentration; and centralization.

- *Rationalization* is seen as a characteristic of distance teaching when the knowledge and skills of a teacher are transmitted to a theoretically unlimited number of students by the detached objectivity of a distance education course of constant quality.
- *Division of labour* is the main prerequisite for the advantages of distance teaching to become effective and is thus a constituent element of it. If the number of students enrolled in a distance course is high, regular assessment of performance is not carried out by those academics who developed the course and other elements of the teaching/learning process are assigned to others.
- *Mechanization.* Conventional education proceeds at a pre-industrial level with the teacher using the tools of the trade (pictures, objects, books) without these changing the structure of teaching; in distance teaching mechanization eventually changes the nature of the teaching process.
- *Assembly line.* In distance teaching the staff remain at their posts but the teaching (manuscript for example) is passed from one area of responsibility to another and specific changes are made at each stage.
- *Mass production.* Traditional forms of teaching envisage small groups and can only be applied to mass education artificially (e.g. a loudspeaker from one lecture hall to an adjoining one). Distance teaching copes confidently with mass production which is essential to it.
- *Planning and preparation.* As in industry, distance teaching is characterized by extensive planning by senior specialist staff in special departments and prior financial investment. Success is linked to the preparatory phase in a way that is different from conventional teaching.
- *Standardization.* A greater degree of standardization is required than in conventional teaching and the educational advantages of the interesting deviation at a particular time with a particular group of students is not possible: the objective requirements of the total course profile dominate the particular interests of the teacher.
- *Functional change and objectification* are further essential elements of the most industrialized form of education, especially when the functional role of teacher is split at least three ways: provider of knowledge (distance unit author), evaluator of knowledge and progress (course maker or tutor), and counsellor (subject programme adviser).

- *Monopolization*. Concentration and centralization are characteristics of the management of distance systems and of industrial enterprise; distance teaching institutions have a tendency to monopolization within a state or national educational provision.

EDUCATIONAL TECHNOLOGY

The completion of this comparative study of distance education and the industrial production of goods led Peters to an analysis of distance teaching in the light of the then current ideas (mid-1960s) about educational technology. He follows distance education through five groupings of educational theorists which he takes over from the German didactician Flechsig:

- simulation models;
- planning models (*Zweckrationalität*);
- materials development strategies;
- systems approach;
- curriculum development.

Peters studies the affinities between distance education and educational technology, especially programmed learning. He shares with Flechsig and the educational technologists of the period the belief that planning and technology will achieve educational success. It was felt that the application of technical categories to educational processes would achieve beneficial results and that systematic planning and rationalization of educational means of reach defined goals (*Zweckrationalität*) could achieve both educational and economic efficiency.

CONCLUSIONS

The final dimension of Peters' analysis of distance education is what he calls the historical, sociological and anthropological perspective. Humanistic attacks on the industrialization of society and its contribution to mass culture lead Peters to expect criticism from humanists of his theory of distance education as the most industrialized form of education.

Tracing the historical evolution of educational structures back to early Indo-European origins, Peters finds them characterized by six elements:

- elitism;
- sacral aspects;
- hierarchical aspects;
- family–small group structures;
- personal communication;
- time–place–person ties.

Distance education is the final phase of the evolution of education away from these sociological structures. It presents a new, strange, and foreign educational pattern that also has six characteristics, being

- egalitarian;
- profane;
- democratic;
- aimed at a mass audience;
- technologically based;
- free from the dimensions of educational time, places and persons.

A sociological analysis based on the German philosophical *Gemeinschaft/Gesellschaft* positions taken from Weber, Tönnies, and Habermas shows that traditional, oral, group-based education follows the '*Gemeinschaft*' categorization with distance education falling into the '*Gesellschaft*' grouping. In general terms '*Gemeinschaft*' structures are friendly and community-based; *Gesellschaft* implies a wider, society-based structure that may be unfriendly. The communication processes within these two sociological groupings show that the intersubjectivity and reciprocity of interpersonal communication in conventional education is radically to be contrasted with the 'context-free', mechanical communication of education at a distance. The possiblity of alienation is not overlooked.

Peters sees as practical consequences of his theory that there is something unnatural about education at a distance. The process of communication is broken up and artificial substitutes for it are provided. The whole communication process is changed and this changes the teaching acts and the learning acts which take place in the education system.

Peters feels that it is a slow process for a teacher to adapt to a distance education system because there will always be clashes between traditional teaching and the carefully structured procedures of a distance teaching university, in which the unity of the teaching/learning process is split into many units performed by different persons and elements of the education system. The process of adaptation however can be furthered by reflection on the characteristics of distance education.

The student in an industrialized education system finds that instruction is available in such ways that he can choose his own way. Instruction is not linked to fixed times, to fixed places, to fixed persons. This throws new responsibilities on the learner that are not characteristic of pre-industrialized education systems.

Peters has no desire to criticize conventional education. His view, however, is that industrialized society of today has developed so many needs for education that it is absurd to imagine that conventional systems can satisfy them. New techniques are needed and these must be industrial.

He recognizes that traditionalists will say: What happens to the highly valued traditions of face-to-face education? What happens to the spirit of the learning community? These are all, he admits, of value but you cannot have 40,000–50,000 students in a system like an open university and try to provide face-to-face tuition with finite means.

Almost alone among distance educators writing about distance education, Peters finds much to query in the industrialization of education. He finds distance education unnatural; it breaks up the process of communication; artificial mechanical substitutes for interpersonal communication are provided; this changes the teaching behaviours and the learning behaviours; there is a definite propensity to alienation. If you are going to teach in the most industrialized form of education, he tells us, you have to be ready to live with the problems that the industrialization of education brings.

It is surely significant that the government of North-Rhine Westphalia decided to locate its open university at Hagen as the wire- and needle-making industries in the valleys of the Hönne, the Ihmertebach, and Oese and the Lenne at towns around Hagen like Hemer, Iserlohn and Altena were the harbingers of the Industrial Revolution from the 1680s onwards. It is an interesting coincidence that the theory of the industrialization of education was developed by Peters who was to become the foundation *Rektor* of the distance university at Hagen.

EVALUATION

Reactions and objections to Peters' thesis have been many and there are those who deplore the introduction of industrial concepts into an educational field. Four of these reactions are considered here: Christof Ehmann, Karl-Heinz Rebel, Manfred Hamann, and integrationist responses.

Christof Ehmann

Ehmann (1981: 231) criticizes Peters' position because of its dependence on faith in the value of planning in education and faith in technical progress. He claims that these faiths, strong in the 1960s, have been shown to be wrong in the 1980s and that 'the application of technical categories to social processes is just as questionable as the use of biological analogies'. Planning euphoria, programmed learning, faith in the calculability of processes – all central features of Peters' industrialized models – have all been dissipated before the 1980s started.

Ehmann's evaluation of Peters' contribution is negative. He feels that as an academic position it is largely dated because of its reliance on theories of planning and technical progress, that its influence on Peters' own institution – the Fernuniversität – has been nil, as has been its influence on the world of commercial correspondence schools.

Karl-Heinz Rebel

Rebel complains (1983: 175) that 'the basis of Otto Peters' assumption – the six interdependent elements that constitute each teaching–learning process (the so-called Berlin Didactic School of Paul Heimann and Wolfgang Schulz) – could never be expressed in such a way that research data capable of falsifying this theory could be collected'.

Manfred Hamann

Hamann (1978) argues that all forms of *Zweckrationalität*, whether they be called media didactics, learning psychology, systems theory, or information theory, have been without success: there have been occasional glimpses of didactic possibilities but no progress towards increased cost-efficiency in education. He accuses Peters of simply applying the structures of Hei-mann–Schulz to distance education and nothing more. This reproach is justifiable for only the didactical analysis part of Peters' presentation. The theory of industrialization is certainly original and owes nothing to Heimann–Schulz either in its presentation or in its origin.

Integrationist criticisms

There are critics of Peters' position who claim that he exagge-rates the difference between conventional education and dis-tance education. Many professors at the Fernuniversität would argue that learning at university level consists of extensive read-ings plus occasional meetings with one's professor, and that distance education is composed of extensive reading plus occa-sional meetings with a tutor.

The long tradition of German university teaching is based on learning from textual materials so that Peters' position tends to overemphasize the difference in the communication process in distance education. Australian systems, in which numbers of students are taught on-campus and off-campus by the same lecturer, reflect a similar position. In some systems each lecturer has responsibility for a defined group of students. For these students the lecturer devises the course, develops the learning materials, sees them through the production process, checks the proofs, marks the assignments for the students when enrolled, provides correspondence and telephone tuition as required, may visit the students either at study centres or in their homes, and conducts the examinations.

Where, representatives of this system ask, is the division of labour, the industrialization, the mass production in this system? Where is the great role differentiation between the lecturer in a conventional and a distance system?

Peters implies that if he were to restate his theory today for the mid-1980s he would change only the references to economic theory and industrial analysis but would maintain the didacti-cal structure of his position. He claims that by substituting more modern economic and industrial references he could produce a theory of the industrialization of education even more convin-cing than what he has achieved so far.

Peters' strength is his knowledge of distance systems as they were throughout the world in the period 1960–5 and the fact that his theoretical positions are clearly grounded in the data he accumulated at that time. The theory also has a certain heuristic value in that it offers some explanation of the nature of educational institutions in which the warehouse and the production process dominate and in which there are few educational installations, and that such systems have a propensity to alienation and monopolization.

Peters' long period as foundation Vice-Chancellor of the Fernuniversität has come to an end since the publication of the first edition of this book. A first collection of his writings was published in English in 1994 and Rumble (1995) has led a wide-ranging discussion of his views on the industrialization of education. Peters (1995, 1996) has replied vigorously, stating that Rumble 'is profoundly wrong when he maintains that distance education is not markedly different from conventional education'. He shows that critics who query his references to the industrial production process neglect the sociological, anthropological, historical and didactic aspects of his work which sees industrialization as a symbol of a new epoch. He is Emeritus Professor of the Methodology of Distance Education in the Faculty of Education, Sociology and Humanities at the Fernuniversität in Hagen.

REFERENCES

Ehmann, C. (1981) 'Fernstudium/Fernunterricht, Reflections on Otto Peters' research', *Distance Education* 2(2), 228–33.

Hamann, M. (1978) *Fernstudienkonzeptionen für den tertiären Bildungsbereich. Analyse des Scheiternsbildungspoiitischer Reformversuche in einem Teilbereich*, Hamburg: Arbeitsgemeinschaft für Hochschuldidaktik.

Heidt, E. (1978) *Instructional Media and the Individual Learner*, London: Kogan Page.

Holmberg, B. (1982) 'Scholarship and ideology: a study of present-day West German educational thinking', *Compare* 12(2), 133–42.

Keegan, D. (ed.) (1994) *The Industrialization of Teaching and Learning: Otto Peters on Distance Education*, London: Routledge.

Peters, O. (1965) *Der Fernunterricht. Materialien sur Diskussion einer neuen Unterrichtsform*, Weinheim: Beltz.

Peters, O. (1967) *Das Fernstudium an Universitäten und Hochschulen. Didaktische Struktur und vergleichende Interpretation: ein Beitrag zur Theorie der Fernlehre*, Weinheim: Beltz.

Peters, O. (1968) *Das Hochschulfernstudium. Materialien zur Diskussion einer neuen Studienform*, Weinheim: Beltz.

Peters, O (1971) 'Theoretical aspects of correspondence instruction', in O. Mackenzie and E.L. Christensen (eds) *The Changing World of Correspondence Study*, University Park, Pa. and London: Pennsylvania State University.

Peters, O. (1973) *Die didaktische Struktur des Fernunterrichts. Untersuchungen zu einer industrialiserten Form des Lehrens und Lernens*, Weinheim: Beltz.

Peters, O. (1995) *Die Didaktik des Fernstudiums: Erfahrungen und Diskussionsstand in nationaler und internationaler Sicht*, Hagen: FeU.

Peters, O. (1996) 'Distance education is a form of teaching and learning sui generis', *Open Learning* 1, 10–15.

Rebel, K.-H. (1983) 'Distance study in West Germany: the DIFF's conceptual contribution', *Distance Education* 4(2), 171–8.

Rumble, G. (1995) 'Labour market theories and distance education: how Fordist is distance education?', *Open Learning*, June, 12–20.

6

INTERACTION AND COMMUNICATION

Whatever a dead teacher may accomplish in the classroom,
he can do nothing by correspondence.

William Rainey Harper, 1880

INTRODUCTION

This chapter presents writers who have emphasized interaction
and communication as central to any concept of distance education. In very general terms Moore, Wedemeyer, and Delling
tended to concentrate on the autonomy and independence of the
student as the basis for their views, while Peters' focus is the
functions of the institution developing learning materials. The
authors in this chapter take as their starting point the role of the
institution in providing a satisfactory learning experience for
students, once the materials have been developed and dispatched.

Five authors have been selected, Bååth, Holmberg, Daniel,
Sewart, and K.C. Smith. Bååth is particularly associated with
an emphasis on two-way communication and Holmberg with a
theory of guided didactic conversation. Daniel, Sewart, and
Smith are, or have been, managers of distance systems. Their
writings are developed from the day-to-day pressure of mana-
ging distance systems. Their inclusion is justified by the wide-
ranging and influential character of their contributions.

TWO-WAY COMMUNICATION

John A. Bååth is Swedish and worked for many years for Hermods at Malmö. His work benefits from a knowledge of the

Table 6.1 Bååth's analysis of teaching models

Model	Two-way communication
B.K. Skinner's behaviour control model	Checking students' achievements; individualizing functions; assess students' starting level; consider special abilities; previous reinforcement patterns
E.Z. Rothkopf's model for written instruction	Helping students get started
D.P. Ausubel's advance organizers model	Determine each students' previous knowledge and cognitive structure; promote positive transfer to subsequent parts of course
K. Egan's model for structural communication	Individually devised discussion comments and 'reverse' assignments
J. Bruner's discovery learning model	Provide individually adapted help; stimulate students' discovery of knowledge
C. Rogers' model for facilitation of learning	Check 'open' assignments for submission; dialogue with each individual student
R.M. Gagné's general teaching model	Activating motivation; stimulating recall; providing learner guidance; providing feedback

Source: Adapted from Bååth (1979)

literature of distance education in the Scandinavian languages, English, German, and French. During the 1970s he was associated with the concept of two-way communication in correspondence education. He would not claim to be the originator of the concept but he made an important theoretical and empirical contribution to establishing this idea as a major defining feature of distance systems today.

One part of his research aimed to relate modern education research to distance education. He examined the applicability of the teaching models of Skinner, Rothkopf, Ausubel, Egan, Bruner, Rogers, and Gagné to correspondence education (which he regards as a subset of distance education) (1980: 12). He was able to show the functions of two-way communication in correspondence education in the light of each of the teaching models (see Table 6.1).

His conclusions are that:

● models with stricter control of learning towards fixed goals tend to imply, in distance education, a greater emphasis on the teaching material than on the two-way communication between student and tutor/institution; and

● models with less control of learning towards fixed goals tend to make simultaneous communication between student and tutor/institution more desirable; this communication taking the form of either face-to-face or telephone contacts (1979: 21).

Holmberg (1981: 27) summarizes Bååth's presentation of the relevance to distance education of the authorities cited in Table 6.1:

● All the models investigated are applicable to distance study.
● Some of them (Skinner, Gagné, Rothkopf, Ausubel, structural communication) seem particularly adaptable to distance study in its fairly strictly structured form.
● Bruner's more open model and even Rogers' model can be applied to distance study, though not without special measures, e.g. concerning simultaneous non-contiguous communication (telephone etc.).
● Demands on distance study systems which would inspire new developments can be inferred from the models studied.

In a second volume, *Postal Two-way Communication in Correspondence Education*, Bååth (1980) adds empirical analysis of two-way communication to the theoretical analysis of his previous book. In particular he studied:

● the relationship of submission density (frequency of assignment submission during a course) to two-way communication;
● the replacement of tutor-marked assignments by self-assessment questions; and
● the introduction of computer-marked assignments as a form of two-way communication.

Bååth's theoretical and conceptual contributions stem from his experience in Sweden. He tells us how his own situation led to his involvement:

When writing correspondence course materials I was struck by the idea that it was possible to provide some kind of two-way communication within the material, by means of exercises, questions or self-check tests with detailed model or specimen answers. Could such two-way communication, to

91

any considerable extent, replace the postal two-way communication induced by assignments for submission?

(Bååth 1980: 11–12)

This combination of personal experience and theoretical and empirical investigation led Bååth to place two-way communication as central to the distance education process and the distance tutor as central to his concept.

Bååth writes well of the importance of the tutor in a distance system. He indicates that there is evidence to show that distance learners need special help with the start of their studies and that they need help in particular to promote their study motivation (1982: 22). He sees the role of the tutor going well beyond that of correcting errors and assessing students' progress:

> This is the role of the distant tutor: he can have important pedagogical functions, not only that of correcting errors and assessing students' papers. He may play a principal part in the linking of learning materials to learning – by trying to relate the learning material to each student's previous reinforcement patterns (Skinner), or to his mathemagenic activities (Rothkopf), or to his previous knowledge and cognitive structure (Ausubel), or to his previous comprehension of the basic concepts and principles of the curriculum (Bruner), or by concentrating on the task of establishing a good personal relationship with the learner (Rogers) – as I have tried to demonstrate.
>
> (Bååth 1980: 121)

Bååth quotes with approval the 100-year-old statement on tutors in correspondence studies:

> The correspondence teacher must be painstaking, patient, sympathetic, and *alive*; whatever a dead teacher may accomplish in the classroom, he can do nothing by correspondence.
>
> (William Rainey Harper 1880)

A query about Bååth's work is that he does not seem to attempt a full theoretical framework for two-way communication in correspondence education. He has greatly furthered our understanding of two-way communication but has not explained how it would fit in an overview of this field. At the time of writing he manages an education consultancy company in Sweden.

GUIDED DIDACTIC CONVERSATION

Börje Holmberg is also from Sweden. In 1995 he became planning president of the new *Fernfachhochschule* (distance polytechnic) at Darmstadt. He has written profusely on distance education in Swedish, German, and English.

A number of characteristic traits link together the publications of Holmberg across thirty years. Among these are a generous, humanistic philosophy that values highly student independence and autonomy, an early concentration on two-way communication in distance education, an emerging concept of distance education as guided didactic conversation, a critical approach to non-print media and the provision of face-to-face sessions as components of a system and a concentration on assignment marking and its importance.

Like the dedicated humanist he is, Holmberg bases his view of distance education on his conviction that the only important thing in education is learning by individual students. Administration, counselling, teaching, group work, enrolment, and evaluation are of importance only in so far as they support individual learning. He would like to see systems with completely free pacing, a free choice of examination periods, and plenty of two-way communication for tutorial and feedback purposes.

Distance education is considered to be particularly suitable for individual learning because it is usually based on personal work by individual students more or less independent from the direct guidance of tutors. The distance student is in a situation where the chances of individually selecting what educational offerings he/she is to partake of can be much greater than that of conventional students. The student studying at a distance can, and frequently does, ignore elements of the teaching package that has been prepared for the course being studied. TV programmes or comments on assignments or face-to-face sessions or visits to study centres may all be ignored.

Holmberg characterizes study in a distance system as self-study but it is not, he insists, private reading, for the student

93

is not alone. The student benefits from having a course developed for him and also from interaction with his tutors and other representatives of a supporting organization. The relationship between the supporting organization and the student is described as a guided didactic conversation. The general approach agrees closely with Wedemeyer's. Holmberg insists on allowing students a maximum freedom of choice in matters of both content and study procedures, individual pacing of the study, and far-reaching autonomy generally.

Two-way communication in writing and on the telephone between students and tutors has been one of his chief concerns. Students' assignments are regarded as facilitators of this communication rather than as instruments of assessment.

Distance education is seen as a guided didactic conversation that aims at learning and it is felt that the presence of the typical traits of successful conversation will facilitate learning. The continuous interaction between the student on the one hand and the tutors and counsellors and other representatives of the institution administering the study programme is seen as a kind of conversation.

There is a kind of two-way conversational traffic through the written and telephone interaction between student and institution. More dubiously Holmberg also argues for what he calls simulated conversation from the students' study of the learning materials that have been prepared in a didactic style.

Holmberg's view of distance education as guided didactic conversation might be presented schematically as in Figure 6.1. There are traces of these ideas in Holmberg's early writings but in recent years he has developed them into the basis for a general theory of distance education.

In *On the Methods of Teaching by Correspondence* in 1960 he wrote:

A considerable portion of all oral tuition can rightly be described as didactive conversation. In a great number of successful correspondence courses the atmosphere and style of such conversation is found. It is typical of the style of didactive conversation that advice is given on how to tackle problems, what to learn more or less carefully, how to connect items of knowledge discussed in different lessons and this also characterises many good correspondence

Figure 6.1 Guided didactic conversation (Holmberg)

courses. It seems to me that advice and suggestions should preferably be expressed in phrases of personal address, such as 'When you have read these paragraphs, make sure that . . .'

(Holmberg 1960: 15–16)

The same paragraph appears with 'didactive' changed to 'didactic' in Holmberg (1967: 26–7) and is repeated in *Distance Education: A Short Handbook* (1974: 27–8) and in 1982 in the revised edition of that book.

Elsewhere Holmberg gives seven bases for his position:

1 that feelings of personal relation between the teaching and learning parties promote study pleasure and motivation;

2 that such feelings can be fostered by well developed self-instructional material and suitable two-way communication at a distance;

3 that intellectual pleasure and study motivation are favourable to the attainment of study goals and the use of proper study processes and methods;

4 that the atmosphere, language and conventions of

95

friendly conversation favour feelings of personal relation according to postulate 1;

5   that messages given and received in conversational forms are comparatively easily understood and remembered;

6   that the conversation concept can be successfully translated for use by the media available to distance education;

7   that planning and guiding the work, whether provided by the teaching organisation or the student, are necessary for organized study, which is characterised by explicit or implicit goal concepts.

(Holmberg 1978: 20, repeated 1983: 115–16)

Distance learning materials developed in the light of Holmberg's theory of guided didactic conversation would present the following characteristics (1983: 117):

- Easily accessible presentations of study matter: clear, somewhat colloquial language, in writing that is easily readable; moderate density of information.
- Explicit advice and suggestions to the student as to what to do and what to avoid, what to pay particular attention to and consider, with reasons provided.
- Invitations to an exchange of views, to questions, to judgements of what is to be accepted and what is to be rejected.
- Attempts to involve the student emotionally so that he or she takes a personal interest in the subject and its problems.
- Personal style including the use of the personal and possessive pronouns.
- Demarcation of changes of themes through explicit statements, typographical means or, in recorded, spoken communications, through a change of speakers, e.g. male followed by female, or through pauses. (This is a characteristic of the guidance rather than of the conversation.)

If a course is prepared following these principles Holmberg (1977) forecasts that it will be attractive to students, will motivate students to study, and will facilitate learning. In two interesting experiments Holmberg rewrote a Fernuniversität postgraduate course on educational planning and a basic Hermods course on English grammar in accordance with his theoretical position and replaced the rather analytical textbook-like approaches of the originals with a more conversational style designed to promote empathy with the student (Holmberg *et al.* 1982).

By any estimation, Holmberg's contribution to the field of distance education is extensive (1979, 1980). His early preoccupation with two-way communication in correspondence education provided an impetus for the research of Bååth, Flinck and Wångdahl in the 1970s.

Although he is not the only scholar to recommend a conversational style for distance learning materials he has been the only one who has developed a coherent theory from his early statement that 'a correspondence course must by definition be something different from a textbook with questions. A correspondence course provides actual teaching by itself and is thus a substitute for both a textbook and the exposition of a teacher' (1960: 8) and then submitted it to empirical testing. In general this position has been beneficial to practitioners in the field and has contributed to making distance learning materials now a recognizably different genre from textbooks.

INTERACTION AND INDEPENDENCE

From 1973 to 1977 Sir John Daniel was director of studies at the Télé-université, Université du Québec, and then Vice-President, Learning Services at Athabasca University in Edmonton, Alberta, Canada. In 1980 he took up the post of Vice-Rector (Academic) of Concordia University, a conventional university in Montreal and moved to Laurentian University, a conventional university with a small distance department in the summer of 1984. He is Vice-Chancellor of the Open University of the United Kingdom at Milton Keynes.

Daniel has thus had experience of academic management in both French and English language distance systems and his thinking about distance education is frequently from a management perspective.

He sees the emergence of distance education systems as coming from three sources: a long tradition of independent study; modern developments in the technology of education; and new theoretical interest in open learning. The fusion of these elements has produced new educational enterprises which teach at a

Table 6.2 Interaction and independence (Daniel)

Independent	Interactive
Reading a text	Discussion on telephone
Watching television at home	Marking and commenting on assignments
Conducting a home experiment	Group discussions
Writing an assignment	Residential summer schools

distance and fulfil important economic and political needs of societies.

When Holmberg and Bååth write extensively of two-way communication in education at a distance they envisage constantly a situation in which the major part of the communication will be by postal correspondence.

Daniel (writing from the start from a university perspective) sees distance systems as comprising activities in which the student works alone and activities which bring him into contact with other people. The first grouping of activities he labels 'independent activities' and the latter 'interactive'. He provides a listing of possible activities in the two groups as in Table 6.2. A major function of distance systems is to achieve the difficult synthesis between interaction and independence – getting the mixture right. All learning in a distance system is achieved by a balance between the learning activities the student carries out independently and those which involve interaction with other people. The balance between the two is the crucial issue facing distance study systems.

The balance chosen between the interactive and independent activities in a distance system has extensive repercussions on the administration and economics of the system. Independent activities, Daniel tells us, have great possibilities of economies of scale since the marginal costs of printing extra copies of texts or broadcasting to more students are low. However, the cost of interactive activities tends to increase in direct proportion to the number of students (Daniel and Marquis 1979: 32).

Increasing the proportion of interactive activities improves student performance, but it does so at a price. The cost of interactive activities is broadly proportional to the number of students involved. There is little opportunity for the economies of scale which characterize independent activities, and which are responsible for the overall cost advantage of distance education.

Daniel states that distance systems should be dearer: things done at a distance usually are. He then parts company from much of the writing on the economics of distance education by stating that there are two economic structures for distance systems: one for the independent activities in which economies of scale are possible; and one for the interactive activities in which they may not be (Snowden and Daniel 1980).

He believes that courses should not be designed that are entirely independent. Socialization and feedback are the main functions of the interactive activities and whereas the importance of socialization in education is less vital for adults studying part-time than for children and those involved in compulsory and full-time education, the feedback role of interaction is of crucial importance. Students want to know how they are doing in relation both to their peers and to the criteria of mastery set by the course authors. Distance students are only weakly integrated into the social system of the teaching institution and feel low involvement with it. Therefore they are at risk and the importance of interactive activities is enhanced.

The thrust of Daniel's thinking on distance education comes through clearly in his attitude to pacing (Daniel and Shale 1979). He suggests that the more freedom a learner has the less likely he is to complete the course. He is of the opinion that distance systems can either give students the dignity of succeeding by pacing them or the freedom to proceed towards failure without pacing. Holmberg, on the other hand, claims that students should be free to pursue distance courses without the pressure of pacing.

Where Moore and Wedemeyer emphasize autonomy and independence of the learner studying at a distance, Daniel looks for a balance between interaction and independence in the structuring of the system and shows how this affects the pacing of students and the cost structures.

CONTINUITY OF CONCERN

David Sewart joined the Open University of the UK in 1973. After a period in the Manchester regional office he moved to the university's central site at Walton Hall near Milton Keynes where he had managerial responsibilities for the provision of support services to students. In 1980 he returned to Manchester as regional director and then returned again to Milton Keynes, where he is at present director of Regional Tutorial Services.

Sewart sometimes tries to trace distance education back as far as the epistles of St Paul but sees a rapid development in the last two decades. This he attributes to the new communications techniques which have been perfected in the twentieth century, the increasing costs of conventional education, and the rapidly expanding range of knowledge.

His theoretical approach to teaching at a distance can be summed up as a continuity of concern for students learning at a distance (1978). Teaching, he tells us, is a complex matter. It is an amalgam of the provision of knowledge and information plus all the advisory and supportive processes with which this provision is normally surrounded in conventional education.

He is unhappy with the notion that the package of materials in a distance system can perform all the functions of the teacher in face-to-face education. He shows that, if it could, it would become an infinitely expensive package as it would have to reflect the complex interactive process of the teacher and each individual student.

In many of his writings he discusses the efforts of course developers in distance systems to produce the 'hypothetically perfect teaching package'. He finds this unrealizable and seeks to prove this with his view of the role of the intermediary in complex civilizations. He argues that just as in most complex bureaucracies an intermediary is necessary (a social worker, a hospital orderly) to bridge the gap between the individual and the institution, so in distance systems an intermediary is necessary between the individual student and the teaching package (Figure 6.2). The intermediary is employed by the institution but works for the individuals in the system and individualizes their problems when confronted with the bureaucracy.

Sewart's clear emphasis on the needs of students learning at a distance, demands an interactive mode in distance systems which can hardly be supplied by the learning materials, however well they are developed. Failure to recognize this has, he considers, led to the almost universal lack of esteem for distance systems which he judges to have been the norm until quite recently. He considers that advice and support for students in

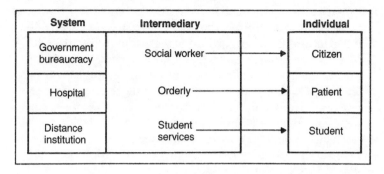

Figure 6.2 Role of the intermediary (Sewart)

a system of learning at a distance pose almost infinitely variable problems and this creates the need for an advisory and supportive role of a distance institution in addition to the provision of a teaching package.

Sewart writes of the differences between conventional and distance education and presents both the advantages and disadvantages of education at a distance. As advantages he lists:

- freedom from the 'strait-jacket of the lecture hall';
- ability to study whenever and wherever desired;
- freedom inherent in the individuality of the distance students' situation;
- student not bound by the learning pattern of a learning group; and
- distance students' needs are not subservient to the needs of a learning group.

The debits are also well presented in Sewart's writings (1981):

- no measure of progress available;
- no framework of study for the distance student;
- no peer group clarification or pressure; and
- no benchmarks on progress or failure.

He considers the situation of the student learning at a distance to be quite different from that of conventional students because of the absence of swift feedback and because the learner's peer group does not act as a benchmark.

101

Whereas the infant school class and the university lecture have easily discernible differences, they are generically similar in offering a group learning situation with a face-to-face teacher/student contact, and the subsequent possibility for instant feedback of an oral and visual nature. The group learning situation is itself supportive of the learning process, not only because of the potential interaction between students in relation to the academic content of the course – learning through discussion with one's peers – but also because the group learning offers a benchmark to the individual members of the group.

(Sewart 1980: 177)

Sewart concludes that the process of learning at a distance is generically different from the conventional mode. The swift feedback available from the face-to-face learning model is almost entirely absent (1980: 177).

The differing study patterns of distance students, the need for intermediaries in complex processes, the absence of the learning group against which the distance learner can measure himself, and the infinite variety of individual problems all lead him to the conclusion that the introduction of the human element is the only way to adapt a distance system to individual needs. This provision should ideally be available whenever and as often as the student needs it and is part of the richness and variety of a system that can adapt to the needs of individualized, independent study. Unlike Peters, however, he clearly sees all education provision as a continuum with forms of distance education fusing into conventional provision.

Sewart's views provide an effective counterbalance to those who see distance education merely as a materials production process. He claims that it is the continuity of the institution's concern for the quality of support in a distance system that has been the Open University of the UK's success in solving the age-old problem of distance systems – the avoidance of avoidable drop-out.

Sewart represents his views in an article published in 1987. There is a continuum, he tells us, between a face-to-face dialogue between one teacher and one student and a 'pure' method of teaching at a distance. There is another continuum between teaching with the complete integration of preparation and presentation by one individual at one end, and the total separation of these functions at the other. The problem is to locate on this continuum the position of the particular distance system that one is analysing or designing.

AN INTEGRATED MODE

When the University of New England, Armidale, New South Wales, Australia began teaching externally in 1955 it adopted a system of integrating external and internal teaching by the full-time faculty of the university. External enrolments were limited on the basis of a staff–student ratio similar to that already existing in the traditional lecture situation so that staff bore responsibility for teaching both student groups as part of their normal duties.

This system (which came to be known as the 'Australian integrated mode') has had two able proponents, Howard C. Sheath (1956–72) and Kevin C. Smith (1973–84). It would be too much to say that the writings of Sheath (1965, 1973) and Smith (1979) contain a theory of distance education; rather they present a series of heartfelt beliefs on how external studies should be administered.

Smith feels that institutions planning external studies must come to terms with an educational dilemma. The dilemma lies in the fact that external studies depend essentially on an independent learning situation and must be designed so that motivated mature-age students can plot their own path through a particular course with a minimum of outside assistance. On the other hand, systems which rely solely upon the stamina, perseverance, and intellectual capabilities of students to survive the rigors of external studies without assistance do not fulfil their academic responsibilities. The compromise is to provide a core of independent learning material but to add compulsory provision for staff/student contacts and regular student group activity.

In contrast to Peters' theory of industrialization, Smith advocates dividing the work of the university faculty equally between on-campus and off-campus students. For the distance education students the lecturer performs all those functions, and more, that are performed for normal students: the design and presentation of courses, the marking of assignments, the conduct of residential and weekend schools, final assessment and examination of students. The external students enrol in the same courses, follow the same syllabus, are tutored by the same lecturers, sit for the same examinations, and are awarded the same degrees as the conventional ones.

Smith bases this structure on the following ideas (1979: 31, 57):

- external teaching should not be done by part-time tutors but by the full-time university faculty;
- by being part of a normal university a distance system remains in the educational mainstream;
- a university has only a small pool of outstanding staff; external students should be in contact with them, not with what he calls 'part-time recruits';
- a university is a community of scholars and all distance students must become part of this community by attending compulsory residential schools;
- concentration on the 'learning package' can lead to a dehumanizing of the learning process, as this is a social experience;
- distance education must not depend solely on correspondence methods. Some degree of interaction not only with materials but also with other students and the teachers is essential.

Smith also lists eight beliefs about how a distance education system should be justified (1979: 54):

1 *Legitimacy*: continuing education and external studies are legitimate functions of universities.
2 *Mainstream activity*: distance teaching should be undertaken by full-time academic staff as part of their normal teaching responsibilities so that it will receive the scholarship, resource allocation, and status it deserves.
3 *Commitment*: commitment is likely if the whole process remains the responsibility of the academic staff and is not divided; personal contact between academic staff and students is required; quotas are imposed to reduce external numbers to the same ratio as on-campus allocations.
4 *Parity*: parity of esteem for degrees can best be achieved if the same staff of the university teach and assess both categories of students.
5 *Interaction*: group discussions between staff and students and between students themselves are beneficial.

6 *Variety*: variety of teaching methods is recommended because of the diversity of students.

7 *Independence/pacing*: pacing of students is a characteristic of successful systems.

8 *Communication*: a distance system requires an adequate administration.

A critique of Smith's position is that he frequently puts forward the particular solutions of his own institution as normative for other institutions. The Australian integrated mode as it evolved at New England is certainly of interest as a model for a small system of less than 5,000 students, but even in other Australian universities which teach both at a distance and on-campus it has by no means been followed in all its details. Far from being in the mainstream of university studies as Smith (1979: 33) claims, the distance departments of many integrated systems appear to be well on the periphery with little influence on university budgets or planning (Rothe 1987).

There is the constant problem that when a lecturer's time is divided between the demands of conventional and distance education, both functions are done less than perfectly (Shott 1983).

If an institution is offering full degrees or diplomas in a non-traditional way it does not seem appropriate that such provision should be located amongst the continuing education and extramural departments which do not normally offer full university degrees (Townsend-Coles 1982: 29–37), yet this is where one normally finds integrated distance departments.

Nevertheless, Smith's contribution is a refreshing one. It is of value to find a thoughtful basis for rejecting concepts of mass production, cost effectiveness, and industrialization in distance education, especially when one finds emphasis placed on bringing the distance student into continuous contact with the best brains of the university and, second, the admission that the education of a distance student should be just as costly as a conventional one. He is at present an educational consultant at Perth, Western Australia.

REFERENCES

Bååth, J. (1979) *Correspondence Education in the Light of a Number of Contemporary Teaching Models*, Malmö: Liber Hermods.

Bååth, J. (1980) *Postal Two-Way Communication in Correspondence Education*, Lund: Gleerup.

Bååth, J. (1982) 'Distance students' learning – empirical findings and theoretical deliberations', *Distance Education* 3(1), 6–27.

Bååth, J., Flinck, R. and Wångdahl, A. (1975–7) *Pedagogical Reports*, Lund: University of Lund (Department of Education).

Daniel, J. and Marquis, C. (1979) 'Interaction and independence: getting the mixture right', *Teaching at a Distance* 15, 25–44.

Daniel, J. and Shale, D. (1979) 'The role of pacing in distance systems', in *The Open University Conference on the Education of Adults at a Distance*, Paper No. 9.

Harper, W.R. (1880) Cited in O. Mackenzie and B. Christensen (eds) (1971) *The Changing World of Correspondence Study*, University Park, Pa.: Pennsylvania State University.

Holmberg, B. (1960) *On the Methods of Teaching by Correspondence*, Lund: Gleerup.

Holmberg, B. (1967) *Correspondence Education*, Malmö: Hermods.

Holmberg, B. (1974) *Distance Education – A Short Handbook*, Malmö: Hermods.

Holmberg, B. (1977) *Distance Education – A Survey and Bibliography*, London: Kogan Page.

Holmberg, B. (1978) 'Practice in distance education – a conceptual framework', *Canadian Journal of University Continuing Education* 6(1), 18–30.

Holmberg, B. (1979) *Fernstudiendidaktik als wissenschaftliches Fach*, Hagen: Fernuniversität (ZIFF).

Holmberg, B. (1980) 'Aspects of distance education', *Comparative Education* 16(2), 107–19.

Holmberg, B. (1981) *Status and Trends of Distance Education*, London: Kogan Page.

Holmberg, B. (1983) 'Guided didactic conversation in distance education', pp. 114–22 in D. Sewart, D. Keegan and B. Holmberg (eds) *Distance Education: International Perspectives*, London: Routledge.

Holmberg, B., Schuemer, R. and Ortmeier, A. (1982) *Zur Effizienz des gelenkten didaktischen Gespräches*, Hagen: Fernuniversität (ZIFF).

Rothe, P. (1987) 'An historical perspective', in D. Kaufman and I. Mugridge (eds) *Distance Education in Canada*, London: Croom Helm.

Sewart, D. (1978) *Continuity of Concern for Students in a System of Learning at a Distance*, Hagen: Fernuniversität (ZIFF).

Sewart, D. (1980) 'Providing an information base for students studying at a distance', *Distance Education* 1(2), 171–87.

Sewart, D. (1981) 'Distance education – 'a contradiction in terms', *Teaching at a Distance* 19, 8–18.

Sewart, D. (1987) 'Staff development needs in distance education and campus-based education: are they so different?', pp. 175–200 in P. Smith and M. Kelly (eds) *Distance Education and the Mainstream*, London: Croom Helm.

Sheath, H. (1965) *External Studies at New England: The First Ten Years*, Armidale: UNE.

Sheath, H. (1973) *Report on External Studies*, Armidale: UNE.

Shott, M. (1983) 'External studies in Australia at the crossroads?', *ASPESA Newsletter* 5(2), 2–9.

Smith, K.C. (1979) *External Studies at New England: A Silver Jubilee Review*, Armidale: UNE.

Snowden, B. and Daniel, J. (1980) 'The economics and management of small post-secondary distance education systems', *Distance Education* 1(1), 68–91.

Townsend-Coles, E. (1982) *Maverick of the Education Family*, Oxford: Pergamon.

Part III
SYNTHESIS

7

A THEORETICAL
FRAMEWORK

Distance teaching: a contradiction in terms?

David Sewart, 1981

A THEORETICAL FRAMEWORK

In this study distance education is an activity which has the following characteristics:

- quasi-permanent separation of a teacher and a learner throughout the length of the teaching process;
- quasi-permanent separation of a learner from a learning group throughout the length of the learning process;
- participation in a bureaucratized form of educational provision;
- utilization of mechanical or electronic means of communication to carry the content of the course; and
- provision of means for two-way communication so that the learner can benefit from or initiate dialogue.

Institutions which organize activities of this kind are called 'distance education institutions' or 'distance education departments' of other institutions. It is claimed that the characteristics outlined above render these institutions distinct from and recognizable from other institutions.

The theoretician confronted with a cluster of activities of this kind needs to address three questions:

1 Is distance education an educational activity?
2 Is distance education a conventional educational activity?
3 Is distance education possible? Is it a contradiction in terms?

Is distance education an educational activity?

There have been occasional suggestions that distance education does not contain any teaching function and therefore should not be classed as an educational activity. Some would wish to classify some distance education institutions with mail-order firms as a subset of business, rather than educational institutions. The data from a number of the institutions in this study showed that they were characterized by:

- input–process–output functions of an industrial rather than eductional nature;
- warehousing, publishing, and dispatch as characteristic functions;
- administration by manager and clerical staff;
- 'teaching' done by accountants, bank officials, lawyers as well as schoolteachers;
- institution oriented largely to production of financial profit.

In spite of these characteristics this study takes up the position that the theoretical underpinnings of distance education are to be found within general education theory. Distance education, the study claims, is a more industrialized form of education but the practice of distance education as evidenced in the second half of this book shows that the educational activities are dominant.

Is distance education a form of conventional education?

Most organized formal education is carried out in classrooms or lecture halls with an individualized teacher in person imparting knowledge and skills to a group of students. It is oral and group-based. The education imparted by such means depends on the availability of teachers at appropriate pupil/teacher ratios in appropriate buildings.

This study proposes that the basis for a theory of distance education is to be found within general educational theory but not within the theoretical structures of oral, group-based education. This is because distance education is not based on face-to-face interpersonal communication and is characterized by a privatization of institutionalized learning. Thus the conclusion of O. Peters, already referred to above, is accepted: 'Anyone professionally involved in education must presume the existence of two forms of instruction which are strictly separable: traditional face-to-face teaching based on interpersonal communication and industrialized teaching which is based on a technologically-produced interaction' (1973: 303).

Is distance education possible? Is it a contradiction in terms?

In the early 1970s Otto Peters set the agenda for a theoretical framework for distance education. He argued that the central theme in the study of this form of education was the justification of the abandonment of interpersonal, face-to-face communication, previously considered a cultural imperative for education in all civilizations, in favour of what Peters considered an apersonal, mechanical, or electronic 'communication' created by the technology of industrialization (Peters 1973).

Writing from UNESCO in the mid-1980s Dieuzeide commented that face-to-face communication remained a cultural imperative for education throughout the world. Distance education constitutes a fundamental break with the educational traditions of most cultures because these are based on face-to-face contact and oral communication (Dieuzeide 1985).

R.S. PETERS AND THE SCHOOL OF PHILOSOPHICAL ANALYSIS

From Otto Peters to today the search for a well-grounded theory of distance education has been an arduous one. Chapters 4–6 have presented the major contributions of scholars from various traditions. It is now time to examine distance education in the light of a generally accepted theory of education to see whether it is possible or contradictory to speak of teaching at a distance or of learning at a distance.

In their 1974 book *Theories of Education. Studies of Significant Innovation in Western Educational Thought,* Bowen and Hobson claim that the English philosopher, Richard Stanley Peters, has made one of the important twentieth-century contributions to the philosophy of education. Richard Stanley Peters belongs to the School of Philosophical Analysis which has been influential in educational thinking in recent decades. This group, which is represented also by Paul H. Hirst and Michael Oakeshott of the

University of London Graduate School of Education, holds that the distinctive function of philosophy is analysis. They see the function of analysis as referring to both concepts and arguments and emphasize the importance of both linguistic and logical analysis.

In this study the analysis of Peters, Hirst, and Oakeshott has been chosen as a suitable basis for the theory of distance education because of the focus of this School on attempting to identify the nature of teaching and learning.

The nature of teaching

Teaching is described by this group of theorists as 'The deliberate and intentional initiation of a pupil into the world of human achievement, or into some part of it' (Oakeshott 1967), and Oakeshott explains that a pupil is a learner known to the teacher and that teaching, properly speaking, is impossible in his or her absence.

These theorists see teaching as a reciprocal act that is impossible in the absence of a learner. One cannot teach without someone being taught. In conventional, oral education this essential reciprocity is clear: if the students do not attend in the classroom or lecture hall, one can speak to the empty room – but that is not teaching. It is also clear that people learn from the day of their birth to their death and that all learning is not dependent on teaching. People learn from books, from television, from looking at the sky. Much of this learning has little to do with educational institutions, whether on-campus or at a distance. In educational analysis, nevertheless, one is concerned only with learning that is the result of communication from a teacher.

Richard Stanley Peters summarizes his views on the relationship between teaching and learning by the concept of 'intersubjectivity' between teacher and learner. In this concept learning is experienced as a conversation or a group experience. Intersubjectivity reflects a shared enterprise in which teacher and learner are united by a common zeal. He describes his concept thus:

> At the culminating stages of education there is little distinction between teacher and taught: they are both participating in the shared experience of exploring a common world. The teacher is simply more familiar with its contours and more

114

skilled in handling the tools for laying bare its mysteries and appraising its nuances. Occasionally in a tutorial this exploration takes the form of a dialogue. But more usually it is a group experience.

(R.S. Peters 1972: 97)

Oakeshott goes further and claims that many of the important aspects of teaching cannot be taught directly. These aspects can only be learned in the presence of persons who have the qualities to be learned. 'How does a person learn disinterested zeal?', Oakeshott (1967) asks. 'How does he learn style, a personal idiom? It is implanted unobtrusively in the manner in which information is conveyed, in a tone of voice, in the gesture which accompanies instruction, in asides and oblique utterances, and by example.'

THE NATURE OF DISTANCE EDUCATION

If the position of this group of theorists has validity, is distance education a contradiction in terms? If the teaching–learning relationship is one of intersubjectivity and basically a group experience in which much is learned by association with those who have the qualities to be learned – can this take place at a distance?

An essential feature of distance education is that the teaching acts are separated in time and place from the learning acts. The learning materials may be offered to students, one, five or ten years after they were developed and to students spread throughout a nation or overseas. In distance education a teacher prepares learning materials from which he or she may never teach. Another teacher may use the materials and evaluate students' learning. The pedagogical structuring of the learning materials, instructional design, and execution may be assigned to persons other than the teacher and to persons not skilled in the content to be taught. Teaching becomes institutionalized: the course may continue in use after the lecturer responsible for producing it has died or left the institution. Materials may be developed by a course team or staff group.

Institutions which use only part-time staff may contract-out the development of the teaching material to writers who are employed only for the period of writing: tutoring and counselling are contracted-out to other staff employed only for the

115

period of the presentation of the course. All of this and much more is the day-to-day reality of teaching and learning in a distance system.

THE REINTEGRATION OF THE TEACHING ACTS

In spite of these realities I believe that a theoretical justification of distance education can be found. It is to be found in the attempt to reintegrate the act of teaching which is divided by the nature of distance education. The intersubjectivity of teacher and learner, in which learning from teaching occurs, has to be artificially re-created. Over space and time a distance system seeks to reconstruct the moment in which the teaching–learning interaction occurs. The linking of learning materials to learning is central to this process. It may be represented schematically as in Figure 7.1.

In conventional education this linking is automatically set up. It may, of course, fail if students sleep or lack motivation, but the learner is placed in a privileged situation totally geared to learning. In distance systems the position is quite different as the link between materials and potential learning has to be artificially maintained. Carefully developed distance teaching materials often fail because they are developed for and dispatched to students who do not open them, or who open them but do not study them, or who study them but do not reciprocate in any way. In a similar way distance education television or radio programmes may go unwatched or unheard, at least by the students enrolled in the course for which they were designed. The link has not been achieved; the essential reciprocity of the teaching act, shattered by the nature of distance education, has not been re-created.

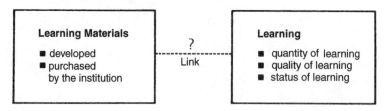

Figure 7.1 Relationship of learning materials to learning in a distance education system

116

INTERPERSONAL COMMUNICATION

In conventional education teacher and learner are linked by interpersonal communication which consists of language and non-verbal communication or cues. Clearly, conventional education uses textbooks and other materials in addition to interpersonal communication, and as the student proceeds from primary schooling to postgraduate study the proportion of printed materials used in the learning process tends to increase. Interpersonal communication, nevertheless, remains central to the teaching–learning process and its functions may be listed as: providing information, expressing feelings, stimulating others, making social contact, controlling others, and functions related to contact seeking and role playing.

Distance education presents a cluster of educational efforts to replace these functions of interpersonal communication by printed, electronic, or computer-based interaction because the interpersonal communication of conventional education is, by definition, excluded except for occasional sessions or meetings.

Distance education has to attempt to compensate for the following differences from interpersonal communication:

- no heard language;
- absence of non-language communication (environmental factors, proxemics, kinesis, touching behaviour, para-language, physical characteristics);
- absence of feedback processes student-to-teacher;
- absence of feedback processes teacher-to-student;
- delayed reinforcement;
- absence of student-to-student communication;
- change in role of non-cognitive learning processes (peer contact, anxiety, peer support, and criticism).

Two studies have analysed the differences between the interpersonal communication of conventional education and the artificial communication processes of distance education. Peters (1973: 295) labels his analysis 'the industrialization of teaching' and Cropley and Kahl's (1983: 37) study is called 'the psychodynamics of teaching at a distance'.

WHAT CAN BE ACHIEVED?

The reintegration of the teaching act is attempted by distance systems in two ways. In the first place the learning materials, both print and non-print, are designed to achieve as many of the characteristics of interpersonal communication as possible. Various writers suggest the incorporation of:

- easily readable style;
- anticipation of students problems;
- careful structuring of content;
- self-testing questions;
- instructional objectives;
- inserted questions;
- model answers;
- typographical considerations: designs, diagrams, and drawings.

In print, audio-visual, video, and computer packages and laboratory kits, authors try to simulate the intersubjectivity of the classroom, tutorial, or lecture.

Second, when the courses are being presented, the reintegration of the teaching act is attempted by:

- communication by correspondence;
- telephone tutorials;
- on-line computer communication;
- comments on assignments by tutors or computers;
- teleconferences, videoconferences, computer conferences.

Many institutions feel that personal contact must be available too and provide for optional or compulsory seminars, weekend meetings, or residential summer schools.

Thus distance institutions are *not* institutions for developing learning materials.

Distance education institutions seek to reintegrate the structure of teaching by providing a complete learning package that parallels the provision of conventional education institutions from pre-enrolment counselling to examination and accreditation. Distance institutions attempt to provide, as well as learning packages, as rich a structure of student support services as is possible to aid the student during the period of enrolment and study.

LE SAVOIR À DOMICILE

Having developed this analysis of distance education in the early 1980s it came as great encouragement to find a reasonably similar approach in the 1985 book, *Le Savoir à Domicile. Pédagogie et Problematique de la Formation à Distance* (Education at Home. A Pedagogical Analysis of Distance Education), edited by Henri and Kaye. This was particularly important because it came from a different continent and from quite a different philosophical tradition.

Henri and Kaye write that 'the pedagogical act is decomposed in distance education over two periods of time and two different places'. They say that the challenge of distance education is to re-create the teaching–learning process. They describe this challenge as follows:

> The challenge which distance education attempts to take up does not lie in the teaching–learning relationship but in the way in which this relationship is achieved in the light of the distance factor. The real challenge lies in the fact that in distance education one has to re-create at a distance the teaching–leaning relationship; one has to put in place from a distance an educational environment in the student's normal living milieu; that from a distance one has to plan, develop and disperse what is to be taught without the possibility of modifying it in accordance with student needs.
>
> (Henri and Kaye 1985: 9)

There seems to be a reasonable similarity of analysis between the French-Canadian book and the approach adopted in this study. Further development under the title 'Reintegration of the teaching acts' (Keegan 1993) was undertaken and evaluation provided by Amundsen (1993) and Sauvé (1993).

THREE HYPOTHESES

In the light of the approach suggested here, three hypothetical positions can be enunciated:

1 The separation of the teaching acts and the learning acts that is characteristic of distance education brings about a weak integration of the student into the life of the institution and

this has been linked to drop-out. It is hypothesized, therefore, that distance students have a tendency to drop out in those institutions in which structures for the reintegration of the teaching acts are not satisfactorily achieved.

2 The separation of the teaching acts and the learning acts that is characteristic of distance education brings about weaknesses in the achievement of interpersonal communication between teacher and student and this has been linked to the quality of the learning achieved. It is hypothesized, therefore, that distance students have difficulty in achieving quality of learning in those institutions in which structures for the reintegration of the teaching acts are not satisfactorily achieved.

3 The separation of the teaching acts and the learning acts that is characteristic of distance education places distance education among the non-traditional forms of education in which degrees, diplomas, and qualifications achieved may not receive full academic acceptance. It is hypothesized, therefore, that the status of learning at a distance may be questioned in those institutions in which the reintegration of the teaching acts is not satisfactorily achieved.

CONSEQUENCES

The process of the reintegration of the act of teaching in distance education brings with it a series of changes to the normal structures of oral, group-based education. Five of the most important are considered briefly.

1 *The industrialization of teaching.* The interpersonal communication of conventional education is replaced by what are basically industrialized processes; the design of mechanical and electronic means of communication, the physical production of printed, audio, video, and computer-based materials, and the distribution of these materials throughout the territory served by the institution or throughout the world.

2 *The privatization of institutional learning.* The learning group is splintered and students study, basically at home, throughout the territory served by the institution. Teaching is focused on the individual student who does not, however, study as a

private learner but as a member of an often complex educational bureaucracy.

3 *Change of administrative structure.* Distance institutions are characterized by two characteristic operating subsystems which have specific task and psychological boundaries: course development subsystem and student support services subsystem.

4 *Different plant and buildings.* The warehouse is central, together with postal or other distribution services. Greatly reduced or spread throughout the territory are student facilities ranging from seminar rooms to library and laboratory facilities.

5 *Changes of costing structures.* Distance systems are characterized by high initial start-up costs, lower variable costs per student and give the potential for significantly lower average costs per student provided the student population is large enough. This represents a move away from the labour-intensive costs of education towards the capital investment structures of industrial enterprises.

REFERENCES

Amundsen, C. (1993) 'The evolution of theory in distance education', pp. 61–79 in D. Keegan (ed.) *Theoretical Principles of Distance Education*, London: Routledge.

Bowen, J. and Hobson, H. (1974) *Theories of Education. Studies of Significant Innovation in Western Educational Thought*, London: Methuen.

Cropley, A. and Kahl, T. (1983) 'Distance education: a psychological analysis', *Distance Education* 4(1), 30–42.

Dieuzeide, H. (1985) 'Les enjeux politiques', in F. Henri and A. Kaye (eds) *Le Savoir à Domicile. Pédagogie et Problematique de la Formation à Distance.*, Québec: Téléuniversité, 29–60.

Henri, F. and Kaye, A. (eds) (1985) *Le Savoir à Domicile. Pédagogie et Problematique de la Formation à Distance*, Québec: Téléuniversité.

Keegan, D. (1993) 'Reintegration of the teaching acts', pp. 113–34 in D. Keegan (ed.) *Theoretical Principles of Distance Education*, London: Routledge.

Oakeshott, M. (1967) 'Learning and teaching', in R.S. Peters (ed.) *The Concept of Education*, London: Routledge & Kegan Paul.

Peters, O. (1973) *Die didaktische Struktur des Fernunterrichts*, Weinheim: Beltz.

Peters, R.S. (1972) 'Education as initiation', in R. Achambault (ed.) *Philosophical Analysis and Education*, London: Routledge & Kegan Paul.

Sauvé, L. (1993) 'Whats behind the development of a course on the concept of distance education', pp. 93–112 in D. Keegan (ed.) *Theoretical Principles of Distance Education*, London: Routledge.

Sewart, D. (1981) 'Distance teaching: a contradiction in terms?' *Teaching at a Distance* 19, 8–18.

8

A TYPOLOGY OF DISTANCE TEACHING SYSTEMS

There are distance teaching universities only in South Africa and the USSR.

Otto Peters, 1965

BACKGROUND

It used to be accepted that distance teaching started in 1840. Holmberg (1960: 3) gives that as the date when Isaac Pitman offered tuition by post in shorthand to students in England. In 1856 Charles Toussaint and Gustave Langensheidt commenced language teaching by correspondence in Germany. Delling (1979: 13), however, has argued that institutions which exhibit all the characteristics suggested in Chapter 3 date back to the 1870s.

Today a listing of distance institutions would embrace most countries of the world and all levels of education.

In previous chapters an attempt has been made to delineate and characterize what has been called 'the farrago that is distance education: open universities and schools of the air; TV and radio projects; government-sponsored institutions prohibited by statute from charging fees alongside profit-making colleges; literacy and rural improvement projects; computer-based instruction and instruction based on roneoed-notes'

A stringent listing of systemic characteristics has been proposed in this book whereby only those institutions exhibiting certain academic and administrative peculiarities, which are reflected in decisions about physical plant, are considered to be distance education institutions for the purpose of this study. Even then the field remaining is vast (Harry 1984) and there is great variety of provision. Global statements about distance education as a whole are rarely valid and most general statements must be hedged with qualifications. The need to provide the reader with groupings or classifications about which at least some general statements may be made with confidence is pressing.

In this chapter some existing classifications which contain elements that contribute to an understanding of the field of distance education are discussed, then a new classification, specially prepared for this study, is suggested.

EXISTING TYPOLOGIES

O. Peters (1971)

The first systematic classification of distance institutions at higher education level was provided by Peters' *Texte zum Hochschul fernstudium*. Peters proposes two major groupings: a western model based on printed materials and correspondence feedback and an eastern model based on printed materials and regular face-to-face sessions. Four bases are given by Peters (1971: 8–12) for his classification: political structure, curriculum structure, organizational structure, and didactic structure (see Table 8.1).

Peters' view that there are two basic forms of distance provision – an eastern one based on printed materials plus consultations and a western one based on printed materials plus correspondence feedback – was not followed by the two other major comparative studies of distance education published in the 1970s. Both the UNESCO *Open Learning* (McKenzie *et al.* 1975) study and the Swedish TRU report (1975) saw broadcast radio and television as central.

The eastern models in Peters' typology were disbanded in the early 1990s, though some aspects of the model survive in China (see Chapter 11).

J. El Bushra (1973)

El Bushra, of the International Extension College in Cambridge, developed a classification of correspondence teaching at universities, comprising the six categories given in Table 8.2. This presentation contains elements of value for an understanding

Table 8.1 Typology of O. Peters

	Western models	Eastern models to 1989
Political considerations	Tries to help the individual	A planned component of socio-cultural development
	Is a fringe form of educational provision	An integral part of national provision
	Characterized by proprietary influences	Enrols 20–50 per cent of all undergraduates
Curriculum	Fragmented provision from individual institutions	Centralized national provision
Organizational structure	Loosely integrated into the mainstream of university life	More influential role in university structures
Didactic structure	Based on proprietary precedents: mono-media system of printed materials plus regular correspondence correction of assignments	Based on imitation of direct education: correspondence correction of assignments is reduced or replaced by regular voluntary or compulsory seminars

Source: Adapted and translated from Peters (1971)

of university distance provision, though a number of groupings chosen are too small for valid use.

M. Neil (1981)

Neil of the Open University of the UK presents a classification of distance institutions based on (1) the degree of authority and (2) the degree of control exerted by the various types of distance institutions in key operational areas (1981: 138–41). The key operational areas are:

- finance;
- examination and accreditation;
- curriculum and materials;
- delivery and student support services.

Neil states that an autonomous distance teaching university is a 'whole system control model' with control and authority over

125

Table 8.2 Typology of J. El Bushra

	Type	Examples
1	Universities dealing exclusively with external students	UNISA, OUUK
2	Universities offering external examination facilities only	External degrees of the University of London
3	Universities offering correspondence teaching in one department only	College of Estate Management (University of Reading) and School of Education; University of the South Pacific University of New England
4	Universities in which teaching departments are required to accept both internal and external students	
5	Universities in which external teaching is provided in a separate department	University of Queensland External Studies Department; University of Wisconsin Extension
6	Universities collaborating to provide instruction on a co-operative basis	Massey University, New Zealand; Texas Association for Graduate Engineering and Research (TAGER)

Source: Adapted from El Bushra (1973)

the four operational areas listed (Table 8.3). Distance departments which are not autonomous but subsections of other institutions are 'embedded into communities of educational agencies' for the purpose of mutual benefits. These 'mixed' models have to share both control and authority in the four key operational areas (1981: 130).

Autonomous distance education institutions clearly have relationships with other education institutions in the nation or state and Neil characterizes these relationships as contractual or commercial. By contrast, distance education departments are embedded in other systems so that mutual benefit between sectors is an important bond.

Chester Zelaya Goodman

The two volume Peñalver–Escotet analysis of distance education *Teoria y Praxis de la Universidad a Distancia* contains a typology of

Table 8.3 Typology of M. Neil

Title	Description	Example
1 Classical centre – periphery model	Whole system control model	OUUK, Milton Keynes
2 Associated centre	An autonomous university with centralized control diminished in area of financing and support services	Universidad Nacional de Educación a Distancia, Madrid
3 Dispersed centre model	An autonomous institution which co-operates with a wide variety of institutions	Coastline Community College, California
4 Switchboard organization model	A facilitating centre for distance education projects with much control exercised by other educational and public bodies	Norsk fjernundervisnung, Norway
5 Service institution model	A service institution based on co-operation with other institutions	DIFF, Tübingen

Source: Adapted from Neil (1981)

distance systems by Chester Zelaya Goodman in his chapter 'La admistración de los sistemas de educación a distancia y sus costos' (n.d. 141–57) as shown in Table 8.4. This is a well-informed and carefully presented typology of distance sytems at university level. The reader will notice how Zelaya accommodates within his structure both the correspondence schools which teach at a distance towards University of London degrees and the co-operative ventures in eastern France, now restructured, and from Tübingen.

Zelaya's category 'conventional universities which offer distance courses which they also accredit' can easily accommodate the sixty-four independent study departments of US universities, the similar structures in Canada, and external studies provision from Swedish and Australian universities. The decision to separate out the CNEC in France as a major provider in an autonomous multi-level distance system is quite justified.

He calls his final grouping the SEAD (Sistemas de Educación a

Table 8.4 Typology of Chester Zelaya Goodman

Title and description	Example
1 Private institutions providing distance teaching for a public institution	Wolsley Hall, Oxford; National Extension College, Cambridge
2 Conventional universities which offer distance courses which they also accredit	Universidad Nacional Autonoma de Mexico; Universidad Xavariana, Bogotà
3 Groupings of conventional universities which unite to offer distance courses	Entente de l'est, France; DIFF, Tübingen
4 Autonomous multi-level distance institutions which teach at university level	Centre National d'Enseignement par Correspondance, France
5 Universities specially created to offer and accredit degrees at a distance	OUUK; UNED, Spain; UNA, Venezuela; UNED, Costa Rica

Source: Adapted from Zelaya (n.d.)

Distancia) and claims that these institutions are totally dedicated to external students. The characteristics are absence of conflicts of loyalty on the part of academic staff between on-campus and off-campus students, greater motivation for methodological experiment; freedom from conventional academic traditions; and – in general – ability to develop new education initiatives for new target groups.

D. Keegan and G. Rumble (1982)

In the preparation of the book *The Distance Teaching Universities*, Keegan and Rumble addressed the problem of the classification of distance systems at university level and came up with the seven basic organizational structures listed in Table 8.5.

CONDITIONS FOR A VIABLE TYPOLOGY

The classification in this study is based on the following premises for the construction of a usable typology:

● It should be helpful to the readers, enabling them to focus on a range of institutions within the field 'distance teaching institutions' about which statements can be made that identify what

Table 8.5 Typology of Keegan and Rumble

Name	Description	Examples
1 Autonomous, centrally controlled distance teaching universities	Open universities with centralized autonomous structures	OUUK; EU; AU; UNED, Costa Rica
2 Autonomous decentralized distance teaching universities	Open universities with some devolution of powers	UNED, Spain
3 Essentially autonomous distance teaching universities operating within a federated university structure	Federal university with both conventional universities and a distance teaching unit	Télé-université of the federal University of Québec
4 Autonomous centralized distance teaching system with a high degree of control using facilities based in and run by conventional universities	Ministry control of distance education departments within conventional universities	Central Office for Distance Education, Dresden, former German Democratic Republic
5 Mixed-mode, uni-departmental model	Special academic distance teaching department in conventional university	External Studies Department, University of Queensland
6 Mixed-mode, multi-departmental model	Academic staff responsible for both internal and external students	Australian integrated mode, New England model
7 Mixed-mode, multi-institutional model	Mixed-mode with responsibility for students at other universities	Massey University, New Zealand

Source: Adapted from Keegan and Rumble (1982)

this grouping of institutions has in common, and what it is that distinguishes it from the other groupings.

- To be helpful it should not be artificial – each grouping should contain dozens, preferably hundreds, of institutions.

- It should not be artificial with regard to students – each grouping should enrol thousands, preferably millions, of students.

- It should not be artificial with regard to time – each grouping should have been identifiable for at least a decade, preferably longer.

- It should try to encompass all distance teaching institutions, public and private, at all levels from primary schooling to postgraduate levels – and not just concentrate on distance education at university level.

- It should only include those distance teaching institutions or departments of existing institutions which exhibit both the major characteristic subsystems of distance institutions (course development and student support services) – for without this limitation the variants are legion. Institutions or departments which are considered not to exhibit both these operational subsystems are excluded (though some of them have made excellent contributions to distance education).

Fundamental to the classification proposed here is the acceptance (with Neil, Keegan, and Rumble) that the basic distinction is between *autonomous distance teaching institutions and distance subsections of conventional institutions* (Figure 8.1). As an explanation of 'autonomous' Neil's (1981: 140) listing of autonomy in (1) finance, (2) examination and accreditation, (3) curriculum and materials, and (4) delivery and student support systems, is accepted as accurate.

It is a question of autonomy at the institutional level because autonomous distance institutions like the Open University of the UK, the Centre National d'Enseignement à Distance in France, and the New South Wales Open Training and Education Network in Australia are components of state or national education systems. Neil explains: 'Although the OUUK is enmeshed in, and utterly dependent upon, the United Kingdom infrastructure, its relationships with other organizations are basically contractual and commercial in nature' (1981: 139).

Once these two basic groupings have been established, further division within the two groupings is by didactic structure, that is the linking structures that the groupings of institutions provide between learning materials and learning. It is when institutions

130

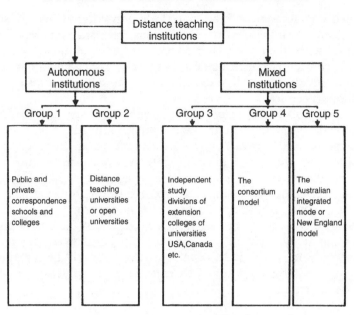

Figure 8.1 Typology of distance teaching institutions

are classified in this way that it starts to become possible to make general statements about the groupings that have some validity. Distance education is too rich and diversified a field of education for more general statements of the type 'all distance institutions do this' to be possible without so many nuances and qualifications as to be virtually unintelligible.

AUTONOMOUS DISTANCE TEACHING INSTITUTIONS

The autonomous distance teaching institutions have been divided into two groups for the purpose of this study. Group 1 is called 'Public and private correspondence schools and colleges' and Group 2 'Distance teaching universities'. The division between the two groups is based on complexity of didactic structure and level of provision.

In very general terms the link between learning materials and learning provided by Group 1 institutions tends to be less complex than by those of Group 2, especially in the use of 'big media' (Schramm 1977) and face-to-face meetings. Goup 1 institutions, whether public or private, sometimes state that students enrol with them precisely because they wish to avoid face-to-face contact. Group 2 institutions sometimes have the intention of supporting the distance learner by as rich a provision of support services as possible.

In terms of level of provision Group 1 institutions normally provide courses for children and adults at lower than university level. Group 2 institutions are called distance teaching universities. The division is not watertight, however, as many Group 1 institutions offer some university-level courses, while most distance teaching universities offer courses below university level.

Autonomous distance teaching institutions that provide a full range of courses from basic adult education to university programmes are of particular importance. Rather than create a new category for these multi-level providers they will be regarded here as having a mixture of characteristics from the two groupings identified.

Public and private correspondence schools and colleges (Group 1)

Correspondence schools and colleges are autonomous distance teaching institutions. They control or have authority over staffing, finance, accreditation, development of materials, and student services even when they are part of a state-wide or nation-wide system.

This model is used widely throughout the world both by government-sponsored and by proprietary institutions. Schools and colleges of this type have existed for over a hundred years and today there are examples in nearly every country of the western world. Examples are found particularly amongst government-sponsored schools at primary and secondary level, and both publicly sponsored and privately supported colleges at technical, vocational, and further education levels. Well-known examples are the National Extension College, Cambridge and Leidse Onderweijsinstellingen, Leiden. In Australia, Canada, and New Zealand this has been the chosen model for government correspondence schools for nearly seventy years, with the Alberta Correspondence School, now Alberta Distance Learning, founded in 1923, reaching 60,330 annual enrolments by 1986.

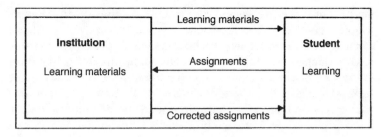

Figure 8.2 A correspondence school or college model (Group 1)

Karow (1979) listed 144 Group 1 institutions (all proprietary) in the Federal Republic of Germany and there must be at least as many in France.

In 1995 more than 5 million students in the United States were enrolled in proprietary, military, religious or government department Group 1 structures (Moore 1995) and an estimated 2.25 million in the European Union in 1994, 50 per cent in government Group 1 structures and 50 per cent in private.

Group 1 is an institutional structure which emphasizes the correspondence element in distance education. It might be represented diagrammatically as in Figure 8.2. The didactic structure is frequently patterned thus: the correspondence schools and colleges develop or purchase learning materials and send them by post to the student. The student studies the materials and posts assignments back to the institution which marks and comments on them and posts them back to the student. The student studies the comments, completes the next assignment and the process is repeated.

Print tends to be the didactic medium with some use of audio-cassettes. From this description and the diagrammatic representation in Figure 8.2 it can be indicated that the environment for student learning provided by this model can be fragile. The student's main contact with the representatives of the institution is by post, so isolation can become a problem.

As many correspondence schools and colleges have a philosophy that suggests that students enrol with them because 'they want to be left alone', it can be maintained that student support services and face-to-face sessions can infringe learner autonomy or the independence of the adult learner. Gone are peer group support and the presence of the teacher. Drop-out can be enormous.

There are, nevertheless, institutions which have turned these disadvantages into factors to benefit student learning. There is evidence to claim (Bååth and Wångdahl 1976; Bååth 1979; Rekkedal 1981; Holmberg 1981: 83–94) that the dedication of the correspondence tutor can forge with the distant student by letter and by telephone such a creative link that a correspondence course can become a form of privileged one-to-one study. A type of one-to-one bonding has often been created that is difficult to achieve in lecture or tutorial.

Distance teaching universities (Group 2)

In 1965 Peters wrote 'The Republic of South Africa and the USSR are the only countries with distance teaching universities.' The scene was quite different thirty years later.

Distance education started the decade of the 1970s as the Cinderella of the education spectrum: it was practically unknown as a segment of national education provision and at times criticized for the malpractice of some of its representatives. It emerged in the 1980s with the possibility of a radical change of image. The foundation of the open universities was a major element in this fairy-tale-like transformation, together with the growing privatization of urban society which characterized the decade and the benefits of industrialization in a period of growing financial stringency.

At the head of the list of distance teaching universities stands the Open University of the United Kingdom (OUUK) at Milton Keynes which received its Royal Charter in 1969 and taught its first students in 1971. Each commentator will have a personal list of the constituents of the OUUK's immediate success, but amongst them were brilliant political and educational leadership, an unswerving concentration on the needs of students studying at a distance and a national backlog of intelligent adults for whom the provisions of face-to-face universities were not fully relevant. These factors and others quickly brought this non-traditional university structure the status of a permanent provider of university education in the UK with an annual enrolment of 200,000.

The OUUK was followed by a series of foundations in both

developed and developing countries of similar institutions called 'Fernuniversitäten', 'open universities' or 'universidades de educación a distancia'. Not only does the foundation of these universities mark a watershed in distance education, it provides the most advanced stage yet in the evolution of the concept of a university.

These universities do not have students in residence, neither do they have full-time day-time students, nor even part-time night-time students. They place their students at home. One looks in vain for students as one walks around the campus at Milton Keynes. Many of the other universities are off-putting, factory-like buildings and there is little or nothing for students to do at them. Gone too is the concept of the university library with places for undergraduate and postgraduate research, gone are the lecture rooms, tutorial rooms, seminar rooms, laboratories for student research, and facilities for the student community.

These are universities of a nation or a state, not of a city like Oxford or Bologna. Frequently they are universities on tens or hundreds of sites spread throughout the nation.

These universities present the most radical challenge yet to the idea of a university enunciated by John H. Newman and developed in the western world. They represent the final democratization of the concept of a university by opening up the possibility of university studies to many who were formerly barred from enrolling by the timetabling of lectures and the necessity of set periods of research at the universities' facilities.

Full-time workers, the disabled, imprisoned, and hospitalized, together with those tied to the home, can now enrol at a university if it teaches at a distance.

In didactic structure, Group 2 institutions attempt to provide a more comprehensive linking between learning materials and student learning. This might be represented as in Figure 8.3.

Distance teaching universities differ from Group 1 institutions in three ways: (1) the level of provision; (2) the use of media; and (3) the more comprehensive link between learning materials and potential learning.

1 *The level of provision.* Correspondence schools and colleges in Group 1 concentrate on education for schoolchildren and

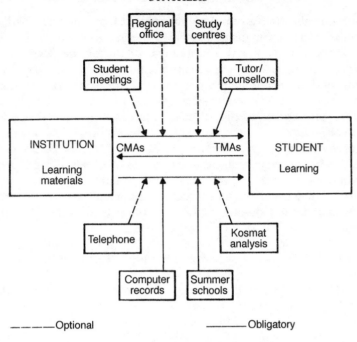

Figure 8.3 A distance teaching university model (Group 2)

further education for adults. The distance teaching universities focus on the provision of university degrees at a distance, though most of the group offer further education courses as well.

2 *The use of media.* A study by Keegan and Rumble (1982: 213) shows a movement towards a more extensive use of educational media by the distance teaching universities. In general Group 2 institutions make a more comprehensive use of non-print educational media than Group 1 institutions.

3 *The didactic link.* Group 2 institutions profess to provide a more coherent link between learning materials and learning so that a satisfactory university-level educational experience is provided.

Multi-level distance institutions

Human institutions do not fit easily into typologies and the autonomous multi-level distance education institutions tend to straddle the two groupings (correspondence schools and distance teaching universities) decided upon.

The Centre National d'Enseignement à Distance (CNED) in France is an example of an autonomous multi-level distance education institution. Today the CNED enrols 350,000 students per year from 170 countries in courses at every possible level from primary and secondary schooling to the equivalent of postgraduate university-level qualifications. The CNED represents a massive, governmental, multi-level provision of distance education on a national basis and as such will be of interest to education planners in both developing and developed countries. The advantages in didactic structure and potential for long-term savings in costs are threefold:

- staff employed on a permanent basis can be used to develop courses at university level, at teacher-training level, at technological level and at other levels in the same discipline and then to update and revise them – thus avoiding some of the problems of tenured academics in Group 2 institutions;
- staff employed as layout artists, audio and video programmers, and instructional designers can benefit from skills learned from working on courses at various levels; and
- instructional designers and plant for media production are all provided once to the same institution and the system does not have to duplicate these installations and staff for each sector's distance department or institutions.

DISTANCE EDUCATION DEPARTMENTS OF CONVENTIONAL INSTITUTIONS

For the purpose of this study three types of a distance education department or section within the structures of a conventional institution have been distinguished. These are:

- independent study divisions of a conventional college or university (Group 3);
- distance education departments of different institutions – the consortium model (Group 4); and
- the Australian integrated mode – New England model (Group 5).

It is felt that these three groupings can be satisfactorily distinguished one from the other both administratively and didactically, though it is clear that they share many common characteristics.

Institutions within each of these three groupings have been in existence for many decades. They have enrolled many tens of thousands of students studying at a distance. Each grouping contains dozens of institutions which teach, normally, at higher education level.

Independent study divisions of a conventional college or university (Group 3)

Examples of independent study divisions are numerous and have been in existence for almost a century. Noteworthy among them are the independent Study Divisions of Extension Colleges of American and Canadian universities. In the 1990s, sixty-four American Universities had independent study departments and there were twenty similar structures in Canada. In France the Centres de Télé-enseignement Universitaire (CTUs) at twenty-two universities fall within this category. In Sweden distance education is organized in this way from a number of Swedish universities. Many universities in India and Latin America have correspondence or distance departments within this category.

Studies have been published of a number of these institutional arrangements, notably by Markowitz (1983) on the independent study departments of United States universities, by Willén (1983) on distance education in Swedish universities, and by Oravep (1994) on France.

One of the administrative structures of these universities is the Continuing Education or Extension College. The Department of Independent Study or Correspondence Study is usually one of the divisions of the Extension College. Departments of Independent Study offer courses in many delivery modes within the field of distance education.

Course development is usually by university faculty paid overload to produce the courses, though a smaller number of faculty (called adjunct faculty) come from other universities and, occasionally, from other sectors of the academeic community. Tuition is also provided by the university faculty and the students study for degrees or certificates awarded by the university.

However, there are limitations on the use of independent study credits for degree programmes in certain departments or schools of the university, and in many cases, one is not permitted to complete a full degree by independent study.

The consortium model (Group 4)

Consortia are groupings of educational and other structures constituted for the organization of distance education. They bring together universities or university departments, government agencies, business partners, radio, television and media production authorities for the purpose of enrolling students in distance education courses.

Examples are the University of Mid America in the United States (McNeil 1993), l'Entente de l'Est in France, the Deutsches Institut für Fernstudienforschung in Germany, the fjernundervisning in Norway, the Consorzio per l'Università a Distanza (Keegan and Lata 1985) and Consorzio Nettuno in Italy, the National Technological University (NTU) in the United States (Davis 1995) and Contact North in Canada (see Chapter 11).

Properly established consortia are more than networks or collaborative arrangements because the members give up some of their autonomy when the majority of the consortium goes against them and because of shared resources. Decisions have to be made on whether students will be enrolled in the consortium or in the individual institutions, and whether the consortium is an award-granting body.

Dunning (1990: 44) claims that one of the most striking effects of the developing role of videoconferencing has been 'the greater receptivity to consortia and partnerships among otherwise non-cooperating, disparate parties', and she lists many distance education consortia in the United States. One of the best known is NTU which started its planning in 1976 as a response to the needs of representatives of leading engineering institutions who, for a variety of reasons, were not interested in enrolling in courses on campus.

In 1983 the NTU was created and in 1995 forty-seven universities in the consortium were offering 1,300 courses for thirteen curricula. The consortium offered 23,000 hours of credit couses in 1994, about two-thirds of which was offered live by satellite, the rest being offered by videotape on satellite (Davis 1995). By 1995 the consortium had awarded 715 masters degrees and had 1,500 students enrolled in degree programmes and 109,000 enrolled in non-credit courses.

'Consortia are only as good as their weakest link' warns McNeil (1993: 129), and the University of Mid America was disbanded in 1982, the l'Entente de l'Est in the late 1980s, and the logistics of offering educational qualifications by consortia have posed challenges to others at both the planning and the operational stages.

The Australian integrated mode – New England model (Group 5)

A distinct form of distance education department within a conventional college or university has evolved in Australia. It is known as the 'New England model' (New England is an area in New South Wales, 300 km NW of Sydney) or the 'Australian integrated mode'. It has been extensively presented: Sheath (1965, 1973), Smith (1979, 1984), (1980), White (1982), Shott (1983a, 1983b) Nunan (1993). It is found, with variations, in Australian colleges of advanced education and universities that teach at a distance. Systems in Zambia, Fiji, Papua New Guinea, and Jamaica have been modelled on it.

There had been a long history of distance education in Australia prior to the founding of the University of New England at Armidale in 1955, but all from Group 1 or Group 3 structures. Individual Australian universities or colleges do not have sufficient distance students to warrant the foundation of an autonomous institution.

In 1955 the University of New England commenced teaching both on-campus and externally. A unique staffing structure and an attempt to preserve as much of on-campus provision for students as possible was evolved for the distance system. The university's lecturers were given a dual mandate and allocated groups of both internal and external students in equal numbers. Lecture notes and even audiocassette tapes recorded live in on-campus lectures were sent to students and a requirement of compulsory periods of time on-campus was built into the distance study programme. This model is presented schematically in Figure 8.4.

The system maintains that the academic staff of the university or

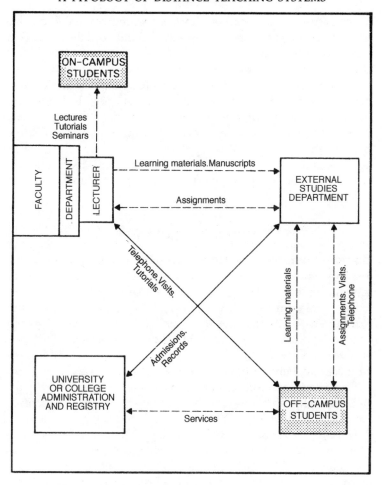

Figure 8.4 Australian integrated mode model (Group 5)

college are to be responsible for the total teaching/learning process of writing courses, teaching them through a combination of independent study materials and face-to-face tuition and assessing the students by way of assignments and formal examinations.

The external studies department is therefore an adminstrative one which organizes for students a series of interactive activities, including at least a brief period of traditional university or college life as a full-time student in residence.

Thus external and internal teaching are integrated. The same academic staff teach and assess both sets of students. Students are enrolled in the same course, take the same examinations, and qualify for the same degrees and diplomas.

Because academic staff have internal teaching commitments to conventional students, besides the responsibility of developing learning materials for external studies and then tutoring them, an External Studies Department is set up to relieve them of administrative details. This department frequently has no teaching function but looks after the production and distribution of course material, student records, statistics, and student support services.

OTHER STRUCTURES

Distance education institutions, as defined in this book, are institutions which teach students. They parallel ordinary schools, colleges, and universities in that they enrol students, teach, assess, and evaluate them and provide a total learning experience for them in every way. They also have a second function, which is not paralleled by ordinary schools, colleges, and universities. They prepare for (some scholars would use the verb 'teach' here too) future students. They prepare printed, audio, video, and/or computer-based learning materials for students who will enrol in the future – next year or in 2–10 years in the future.

The demands of a viable typology that would comprise groupings of institutions large enough for practical use has eliminated from consideration a number of institutions that are often associated with the evolution of distance education. These include (1) some accrediting institutions; (2) some materials production centres; and (3) certain audio–video, television and multi-media programmes.

CONCLUSION

In this chapter a classification has been provided for those institutions characterized by all the characteristics of distance education institutions outlined in the previous chapters. Within the unity of distance education, a major difference was claimed betwen autonomous distance education institutions and distance departments of conventional institutions. Within these two groupings further subdivisions were indicated to arrive at groupings of institutions about which general statements can be made with confidence.

REFERENCES

Bååth, J. (1979) *Postal Two-Way Communication in Correspondence Education*, Malmö: Liber Hermods.

Bååth, J. and Wangdål, A. (1976) 'The tutor as an agent of motivation in correspondence education', *Pedagogical Reports*, No. 8, University of Lund.

Davis, S. (1995) 'Speaking personally with Lionel Baldwin', *The American Journal of Distance Education* 9(2) 76–81.

Delling, R. (1979) Lehrbrief als Fernlehrgelegenheit, *ZIFF Papiere*, Hagen: Fernuniversität.

Duning, B. (1990) 'The coming of the new distance educators in the United States. The telecommunications generation takes off', *Distance Education* 11(1), 24–49.

El Bushra, J. (1973) *Distance Teaching at University Level*, Cambridge: IEC.

Harry, K. (1984) 'The International Centre for Distance Learning's new computerised database', *ICDE Bulletin* 6, 6–7.

Holmberg, B. (1960) *On the Methods of Teaching by Correspondence*, Lund: Gleerup.

Holmberg B. (1981) *Status and Trends of Distance Education* London: Kogan Page.

Karow, W. (1979) *Private Fernunterricht in der Bundesrepublik Deutschland und in Ausland*, Berlin: DIBB.

Keegan, D. and Lata, F. (eds) (1985) *L'università a distanza. Riflessioni e proposte per un nuovo modello di università*, Milan: Angeli.

Keegan, D. and Rumble, G. (1982) 'Distance teaching at university level', in G. Rumble and K. Harry (eds) *The Distance Teaching Universities*, London: Croom Helm.

McKenzie, O., Postgate, R. and Scupham, J. (1975) *Open Learning*, Paris: UNESCO.

McNeil, D. (1993) 'The rise and fall of a consortium: the story of the Univesity of Mid-America', pp. 123–31 in L. Moran and I. Mugridge (eds) *Collaboration in Distance Education*, London: Routledge.

Markowitz, H. (1983) 'Independent study by correspondence in American universities', *Distance Education* 4(2), 149–70.

Moore, M. (1995) 'American distance education: a short literature review', in F. Lockwood (ed.) *Open and Distance Learning Today*, London: Routledge.

Neil, M. (1981) *The Education of Adults at a Distance*, London: Kogan Page.

Nunan, T. (ed.) (1993) *Distance Education Futures*, Adelaide: Univesity of South Australia.

Oravep (1994) *Formations ouvertes et à distance: la situation en France*, Paris: Oravep.

Peñalver, A. and Escotet, M. n.d. *Teoria e Praxis de l'Universidad a Distancia*, San Jose: UNED.

Peters, O. (1965) *Der Fernunterricht*, Weinheim: Beltz.

Peters, O. (1971) *Texte zum Hochscul fernstudium*, Weinheim: Beltz.

Rekkedal, T. (1981) *Introducing the Personal Tutor Counsellor in a System of Distance Education*, Stabbek: NKI Norway.

Schramm, W. (1977) *Big Media, Little Media*, London: Sage.

Sheath, H. (1965) *External Studies at New England: The First Ten Years*, Armidale, NSW: UNE.

Sheath, H. (1973) *Report on External Studies*, Armidale, NSW: UNE

Shott, M. (1983a) 'External studies in Australia at the crossroads?' *ASPESA Newsletter* 9(2), 2–9.

Shott, M. (1983b) 'Final report to the ASPESA executive', *ASPESA Newsletter*, 9(3), 15–17.

Smith, K.C. (1979) *External Studies at New England: A Silver Jubilee Review 1955–1979*, Armidale, NSW: UNE.

Smith, K.C. (1984) *Diversity Down Under in Distance Education*, Toowoomba, Queensland: Darling Downs IAE.

TRU report (1975) *An Analysis of Distance Systems*, Stockholm: SOU.

White, M. (1982) 'A history of external studies in Australia', *Distance Education* 4(2), 101–21.

Willén, B. (1983) 'Distance education in Swedish universities', *Distance Education* 4(2), 211–22.

Zelaya Goodman, C. (n.d.) 'La administración de los sistemas de educación a distancia y sus costos, in A. Peñalver, and M. Escotet, *Teoria e Praxis de l'Universidad a Distancia*, San Jose: UNED 1, 141–57.

9

PLANNING DISTANCE SYSTEMS

The motion picture is the great educator of the poorer people. It incites their imagination by bringing the whole world before their eyes. It sets spectators thinking and raises their standard of living. Books will soon be obsolete in the public schools. Scholars will be instructed through the eye. It is possible to teach every branch of human knowledge with the motion picture. Our school system will be completely changed inside of ten years.

Thomas A. Edison, 1913

The typology developed in the previous chapter gives a basis for planning for distance education. Each of the five models identified has a theoretical framework and numerous examples in the world of distance education today.

AN AUTONOMOUS INSTITUTION OR A SUBSECTION OF A CONVENTIONAL ONE?

The first question to be addressed by administrators or education planners is whether to choose an autonomous distance institution or a distance subsection of an existing school, college, or university. Sewart (1986) addresses this question in an article 'Single mode versus dual mode: a fair question?' His conclusion is that distance systems now in existence are single mode or dual mode because of historical accident and external factors rather than as a result of educational debate (1986: 15).

In *The Distance Teaching Universities* (1982: 245) Keegan and Rumble initiated the educational debate and proposed planning

145

guidelines which are still relevant. In general terms the conclusion of that study was that in systems where there are less than 10,000 enrolments per year one is naturally inclined towards a department of an existing institution; but that beyond 20,000 enrolments a distance teaching school, college, or university is the favoured solution. Further analysis took place in 1992 and 1994 (Rumble, 1992; Keegan 1994).

The final decision for educational planners will depend on a detailed theoretical knowledge of distance education; costs (see chapter 10); and a detailed knowledge of the social, political, historical, and educational structures of the region in question.

AN AUTONOMOUS INSTITUTION

Large distance institutions like the 350,000 Centre National d'Enseignement à Distance in France with 350,000 students from 170 countries in 1995 or Sukkhothai Thammatirat Open University in Bangkok with 350,000 students in 1995 have no need for conventional face-to-face students. Where would they put them? Their whole cost structures are built on the premise that they do not have to build buildings for students.

In the same way the full-time staff of such institutions are fully occupied in designing floppy disks, video, audio, and printed materials for future students, together with the teaching at a distance of students presently enrolled in courses previously developed. One cannot realistically expect such staff to take on in addition a third major area of didactic activity: lecturing in lecture halls and providing tutorials for face-to-face students.

If the choice is in favour of a separate distance institution then one has to consider the advantages of the correspondence school model (Group 1) or the distance teaching university model (Group 2) or a multi-level structure.

Group 1 models

Most proprietary institutions are Group 1 models (Glatter and Wedell 1971; Weinstock 1976; Karow 1979). Some are quite small, well below the 10,000 enrolments recommended by Keegan and Rumble (1982), but have existed happily for decades.

Some Group 1 government institutions in Australia, Canada, and New Zealand have less than 10,000 enrolments but have survived successfully for 60–70 years. Some are quite large: the New South Wales Open Training and Education Network, formerly the New South Wales College of External Studies, had 30,000 students in 1995, the Open Polytechnic of New Zealand, formerly the Technical Correspondence School, had 40,000 and Alberta Distance Learning, formerly the Alberta Correspondence School, 16,000

Group 2 models: the distance teaching universities

Dodd and Rumble (1984) have analysed the planning process when the choice falls on a distance teaching university. In a study that ranges widely from Nigeria to Costa Rica and Japan they leave the impression that the personal view of particular politicians played a decisive role in the period from the Report of the National Planning Committee (a stage in most developments in the study) to the creation or abandonment of the project.

Most of the open universities studied in the 1982 book *The Distance Teaching Universities* quickly reached the 10,000 volume suggested by Rumble and Keegan. Some, like the Asian foundations of the 1980s, are very large with hundreds of thousands of students. Athabasca University, in Northern Alberta, has had difficulties reaching the suggested size but has survived nevertheless.

Of particular importance to students is the planning of the Open Universeit in the Netherlands (Chang *et al.* 1983). This is a distance teaching university in a country with minimal distances and an excellent network of universities that raced to 50,000 enrolments soon after its inception.

The Open University of Tanzania was founded in 1993, the Open University of Bangladesh in 1994 and the Open University of Catalonia, planned as the world's first public virtual university, in 1995.

A DEPARTMENT OF AN EXISTING INSTITUTION

There are three basic models if the choice is for a department of an existing institution. These models are normally found in publicly funded institutions at university and college level, rather than proprietary ones.

147

Group 3 models: correspondence study departments

Models for analysis abound. Group 3 is a frequent choice for distance education in higher education institutions in the United States of America, Canada, France, Sweden, India and South America.

For the student and the planner the 1983 article by Markowitz 'Independent study by correspondence in American universities' will provide a useful introduction, as will a subsequent article by the same author on the costing of such departments (Markowitz 1987).

Group 4: the consortium model

A planning option in certain circumstances is for a grouping of institutions to form a consortium for the development of distance education courses and the enrolment of distance students. The planning of a distance university system for Italy in 1983 was confronted by the impossibility of the parliament legislating for a distance university (Group 2) and by the problem that centuries of Italian university legislation made Groups 3 or 5 untenable.

The solution found was a consortium. Basically this was a business structure which paid leading academics to write distance learning materials as if they were writing a book. Students enrolled in one of the universities which joined the consortium. The consortium organized student support services and paid tutors, but the students returned to the universities for the examinations as conventional students (Keegan and Lata 1985).

Group 5: the New England model

Among the options available when the choice is for a department of an existing school, college, or university is the Group 5 structure sometimes referred to as the New England model or the Australian integrated mode.

The fundamental difference between Group 5 structures and those of Groups 3 and 4 is the changes that the distance department occasions in the structure of the rest of the university. Staffing workloads, departmental priorities, and costings are modified in this model to enable full-time faculty to teach both on-campus and off-campus students. Whether planners can consider a Group 5 structure will depend on university legislation and tradition in their state or nation.

STUDENTS

Detailed analyses of distance students have been published by many institutions. Planners of distance systems will be concerned with the characteristics of distance students and the retention of students in the system.

Characteristics

A major grouping of students who have chosen to study at a distance is the enrolment of the Open University of the UK. A detailed analysis of these students undertaken by Field (1982) identifies four characteristics which differentiate these students from the traditional university undergraduate in Britian: experience, aspirations, study milieu, and investment.

The major findings of Field's analysis of OUUK students and university students in general might be presented as in Table 9.1. In general distance students tend to be gainfully employed, have less prior education, are older, and live comparatively far away from the nearest place offering the same course in a different form.

Privatization of the study process and isolation from teacher and peer group remain the central distinctive features of distance students. These are factors that make studying at a distance a perilous task for those who cannot benefit from privacy.

Drop-outs

Preoccupation about drop-outs is a constant feature of distance education literature and practice, though *not* at primary and secondary school level. A possible theoretical basis for an analysis of drop-out in distance education might be an adaptation of Tinto's work on drop-out in on-campus courses to the problem of studying at a distance. Tinto developed a theoretical model, based ultimately on Durkheim, in which it was hypothesized that weakness of integration of the student into the social fabric

Table 9.1 Differences between OUUK students and other university students

Students generally	OU Students
1 Experience	
People under 25, with little direct experience of employment; of the application of knowledge or techniques in service or industrial settings; of human relations or of social changes	75 per cent aged 30–55 with a diverse accumulation of experience; with ideas on evidence, accuracy and analysis not gained from schooling. For many learning starts with unlearning
2 Aspirations	
People locked into education because of selection and training; because of family expectations; because of tied income and for whom in the current economic climate there is no attractive alternative	For some, university studies are central as there is no other way to fulfil aspirations; or study gives a new dimension to existing work; or study is marginal with family and job responsibilities dominating it
3 Study milieu	
Easy access to learning media; to fellow students; to advisors and tutors; leisure facilities are complementary to study; all within a convenient distance	The study milieu is generally characterized by its distance from the source of instruction; the distance in time caused by the mismatch between student-system time and institutional time
4 Investment	
Traditionally a paid-for place in an institution of higher education has been the surest route to a clean, pleasant and interesting job. More recently it is a postponing of unemployment or work experience. Graduates emerge not very useful to employers but they can be developed and exploited by employers	The student takes on and finds money for an extra workload, a departure from most of his peers. To the family of the student the return may be less tangible than from other activities. The graduates are older, expensive and less mobile but with extensive experience of life

Source: Adapted from Field (1982)

of the institution was an indicator of possible drop-out (Sweet 1986).

If one were to accept this theory, virtually all distance students would be 'at risk'. Their integration into the stucture of their university or college is fragile and continually so throughout the length of the study programme. The distance student, almost by definition, does not take part in the life of the institution and the industrialization of distance systems works to produce a customer/business atmosphere which negates the integrative support mechanisms which Tinto hypothesizes as vital. The privatization of learning at a distance tends further to provoke lack of integration.

This study suggests that there is a propensity to drop out by enrollees in distance education. This propensity can be attenuated by the planning of quality learning materials but above all by the provision of adequate student support services for the avoidance of avoidable drop-out. Where student support of an adequate nature is not provided, students should understand that distance study may be constantly fraught with the risk of discontinuation.

Time

Time available for study is closely related to success or failure in distance education; it is also closely related to drop-out. The German scholar Schwittmann studied the relation between time available for study and success at both the Funkkolleg programmes by radio in Southern Germany and the courses at the Fernuniversität in North-Rhine Westfalen.

Schwittmann (1982) claims that 'time available for study' is the only important variable for predicting success or failure in a distance study programme. He goes further and forecasts that from a multi-media study package (including visitis to study centres, watching television programmes, listening to radio programmes, studying course materials, doing assignments) one can forecast which element of the multi-media study package will be dropped first when one knows the relevance of each element towards the final examination and the amount of time available to the student.

When distance study is completed in company time or as part of a work programme, there seems to be little or no drop-out from distance courses.

COURSES

Holmberg (1981: 14, 49) has shown that most subject areas can be taught at a distance, whether in terms of Bloom's taxonomy or of the learning styles of Marton and Säljö.

Questions for planners arise concerning the status and accreditation of the courses chosen. Study at a distance is arduous (chapter 4). The status of learning at a distance is fragile (chapter 7). There is little purpose in studying at a distance for years to gain a degree or a diploma if you then find that the degree or diploma is not valid for further study or has little status with managers at employment interviews.

Status for distance awards depends in large measure on the acceptance of the theoretical basis for distance education by faculty members of university education departments and on the acceptance by vice-chancellors and senior administrators of conventional institutions of the validity of qualifications won at a distance.

Accreditation

The quality of distance courses and their accreditation contribute to the status of distance courses.

A national system of accreditation of degrees and diplomas at all levels, as in France, works in favour of a distance system. Such a system is however, often criticized as lacking in freedom and flexibility. It works, none the less, in favour of the distance system as there is instant status and national accreditation for the study at a distance.

Similarly in Italian universities examinations are oral, and this system can cause problems for commentators from other backgrounds. It seems, none the less, quite appropriate that students who have studied for university qualifications at a distance should be examined face to face.

Group 1 government-sponsored institutions are usually accredited as the distance component of nation-wide systems. Group 1 privately supported institutions are usually monitored by national associations like the DETC in the United States of America and the Association of European Correspondence Schools, both of which have gained in stature in recent decades.

Group 2 institutions, like other universities, have accreditation built into their charters. Some, in addition, appoint external examiners.

Group 3 institutions participate in the university or college accreditation of their respective countries, though some distance departments have difficulty in winning accreditation for the award of whole degrees at a distance, especially at postgraduate level.

Group 5 institutions usually have little trouble with accreditation as they participate in the award structure of their college or university, with students sitting for the same assessment procedures as on-campus students in the same courses.

CHOICE OF MEDIUM

Literature

This is the area of the field of distance education study which has been most widely researched and on which the volume of publication is most rapidly increasing. There are authoritative overviews (Bates 1995) and guides to good practice (Rowntree 1991) which will be of value to planners of new systems in all countries.

History

Distance systems have dealt with the use of media in education for over a hundred years but the evidence for the whole of the period has rarely been subjected to analysis. From time to time there have been forecasts like that of Edison in 1913 in favour of the cinematograph, that one medium would come to dominate either on-campus or off-campus, but this has never been realized. There is often a mismatch between the literature and the practice of distance institutions, which is determined by costs, course shelf-life and media which have been purchased at the time of course development.

Context

Planners of distance systems approach the choice of media with decisions to be made on the quantity of education to be achieved (the avoidance of avoidable drop-out), the quality of student learning to be achieved, the status of the system and costs. Rumble has shown (see chapter 10) that the effect of choice of medium on the costs of a system is permanent.

What medium, then, should be chosen? It often comes as a surprise to those who do not know distance systems that there are two answers to the question. The choice of media to carry the content of the course may be quite different from the media chosen for the presentation of the course to students, often many years later. Print may be a good choice of medium for the content of many courses (Landry 1985), but when the course is being studied by students they may need rapid feedback by telephone, electronic mail, computer-, or videoconferencing (Holmberg 1984: 50). A comprehensive guide to the choice of synchronous technologies for inclusion in distance systems has been provided by Portway and Lane (1994).

ADMINISTRATION

Miller and Rice (1967) in their *Systems of Organisation. The Control of Task and Sentient Boundaries*, show how organizations can be characterized by their essential operating activities and show the importance of analysing task boundaries and sentient (personal) boundaries in administration. In Miller and Rice's terms it is important to identify the 'operating activities' that characterize the enterprise. The operating activities are those that directly contribute to the import/conversion/export processes which define the nature of the enterprise and differentiate it from other enterprises.

Miller and Rice's theory of system organization was applied to the organization of distance education systems by Kaye and Rumble (1981). They had little difficulty in identifying two characteristic operating subsystems, 'course development' and 'student support services', and the task boundaries that separate these activities within the organization from other activities (see Figure 9.1). The *course development subsystem* comprises the planning, designing, crystallizing, and recording of the teaching (together with the proposed methodologies and structures for presenting the teaching at a future date) in mechanical or electronic form. The *student support subsystem* comprises the activities designed by the institution to focus on the student's home

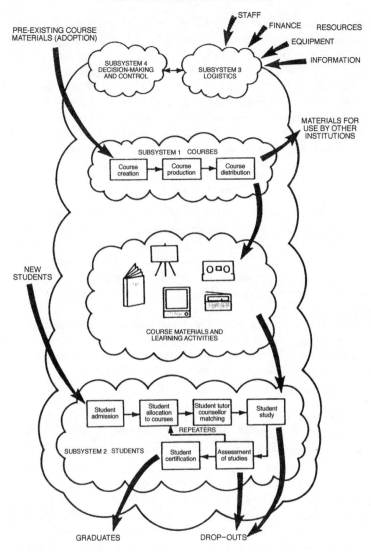

Figure 9.1 Administrative subsystems in a distance education system
Source: Reproduced with permission from Kaye and Rumble (1981)

(or institutional centre near the student's home) that will provide a private and individualized presentation of the pre-
recorded course content, together with the simulation of teacher

and peer-group clarification, that normally accompany the presentation of courses in oral, group-based educational provision.

Distance education enterprises have clusters of task and sentient boundaries which focus on the process of 'course development' and others which focus on the process of 'support services for students studying at home' in a way which cannot be found in other educational institutions. These two charactersitic operating subsystems define the nature of a distance system and differentiate it from other forms of educational adminstration.

Course development

Course development for distance education implies the preparation of print and non-print materials plus the production of a total learning experience for the distance student that will parallel all the facilities that are characteristic of on-campus education, including additional homework, laboratory practicals, and library research periods and all the activities of face-to-face study.

The adminstration of course development procedures gives a range of possibilities from the single author to the course teams of the OUUK which often have more than twenty members from OUUK full-time staff, BBC staff and consultants from business or other universities.

Student support services

The provision of student support services achieves for distance systems the essential feedback mechanisms that are characteristic of education. It is mainly through them that two-way communication is established between student and institution, though the better course materials have inherent feedback mechanisms as well. Provision of student support services distinguishes distance education institutions from publishing houses and other producers of learning materials.

The five major goupings in the typology developed for this book have, in general, different approaches to the provision of student support services. One of the groupings of institutions has heavy involvement in this provision: Group 5, the Australian integrated mode. Two groupings of institutions have tended to rely on the development of learning materials as central, with student support focusing on attentive correction and comment on assignments: Group 1, the correspondence schools and colleges; and Group 3, the independent study model. Groups 2 and 4 (the autonomous distance teaching universities model and the consortium model) vary widely in theoretical and financial commitment to student support services.

PLANNING FOR THE FUTURE

In the distance education university of the mid-1990s the lecturer sits all day long at his or her word processor. The content of the course is input into the word processor and the lecturer prints out a hard copy from the printer. No secretary or typing pool support is used and the need to proofread for other person's errors is eliminated. The lecturer corrects the hard copy, puts in the corrections and prints out a final version of the course materials to ensure that the text is correct. He or she then inserts the university's house style instructions for headings, subdivisions, choice of typeface, and layout.

The lecturer then turns to his or her mouse to prepare the computer-designed illustrations, graphs, diagrams, and other illustrative features that he or she wishes to use as part of the teaching. When these are completed to the lecturer's satisfaction, they are blended electronically into the text. The text and illustrations are printed out and the printed materials for the course are now complete.

The materials can be distributed to the students' computers by satellite and the student can decide whether to study them on screen or print a hard copy. Alternatively the materials can be photocopied or plates can be made for conventional printing. The whole process of teaching at a distance has been industrialized and rationalized with the elimination of intermediary persons between the lecturer and the students.

As the lecturer spends much of his or her time at the word processor or in the audio, video, or computer design laboratory when not working at the word processor, the teaching style of the distance education lecturer has evolved far from that of the on-campus university and the skills and training required are quite different. The lecturer needs the skills of a word-processor operator, of an instructional designer, graphic artist, and layout expert for print materials and extensive skills in the development and evaluation of audio, video and computer-based materials.

Distance education professionals will face further planning decisions in the future as they seek to assess the cost-effectiveness and educational-effectiveness of the inclusion of the new range of telecommunications technologies in distance systems, ranging from the Internet to the use of the two-way video window on a growing range of computers and the availability of multi-media systems in the home.

REFERENCES

Bates, A. (1995) *Technology, Open Learning and Distance Education*, London: Routledge.

Chang, T., Crombac, H., van der Drift, K and Moonen, J. (1983) *Distance Learning. On the Design of an Open University*, Boston: Kluwer-Nijhoff.

Dodd, J. and Rumble, G. (1984) 'Planning new distance teaching universities', *Higher Education* 13(3), 171–97.

Edison, Thomas Alva (1913) 'The evolution of the motion picture (interview with Frederick James Smith)', *The New York Dramatic Mirror*, 9 July, 24–5.

Field, J. (1982) 'Characteristics of OU students', *Teaching at a Distance Research Supplement* (No. 1), Milton Keynes:

Glatter, R. and Wedell, E. (1971) *Study by Correspondence*, London: Longman.

Holmberg, B. (1981) *Status and Trends in Distance Education*, London: Kogan Page.

Holmberg, B. (1984) 'On the educational potentials of information technology with special regard to distance education', *ICDE Bulletin* 6, 49–54.

Karow, W. (1979) *Privater Fernunterricht in der BDR und in Ausland*, Berlin: BIBB.

Kaye, A. and Rumble, G. (1981) *Distance Teaching for Higher and Adult Education*, London: Croom Helm.

Keegan, D. (1994) 'The competitive advantages of distance teaching universities', in *Open Learning* 9(2), 36–9.

Keegan, D and Lata, F. (1985) *L'Università a Distanza*, Milan: Angeli.

Keegan, D. and Rumble, G. (1982) 'The distance teaching universities: an appraisal', in G. Rumble and K. Harry (eds) *The Distance Teaching Universities*, London: Croom Helm.

Landry, F. (1985) 'L'imprimé: un moyen d'enseignement privilégié, pp. 209–59 in F. Henri and A. Kaye *Le Savoir à Domicile*, Québec: Télé-université.

Markowitz, H. (1983) 'Independent study by correspondence in American universities', *Distance Education* 4(2), 149–70.

Markowitz, H. (1987) 'Financial decision making – calculating the costs of distance education', *Distance Education* 8(2), 147–60.

Miller, E. and Rice, A. (1967) *Systems of Organisation. The Control of Task and Sentient Boundaries*, London: Tavistock.

Portway, P. and Lane, C. (eds) (1994) *Guide to Teleconferencing and Distance Learning*, San Ramon Calif. Applied Business Telecommunications.

Rowntree, D. (1991) *Teaching through Self-instruction*, London: Kogan Page.

Rumble, G. (1992) 'The competitive vulnerability of distance teaching universities', *Open Learning*, June, 31–45.

Schwittmann, D. (1982) 'Time and learning in distance education', *Distance Education* 3(1), 155–71.

Sewart, D. (1986) 'Single mode versus dual model: a fair question?', *Open Campus* 12, 10–15.

Sweet, R. (1986) 'Student drop-out in distance education: an application of Tinto's model', *Distance Education* 8(2), 201–19.

Weinstock, N. (1976) *Les Cours par Correspondance du Secteur Privé en Belgique*, Brussels: Centre National de Sociologie du Droit Civil.

Part IV

EVALUATION

10

ECONOMICS

'Put yourself in my place', said the Minister. 'You're asking me to make a tough decision, but you're not giving me the facts.'

The Secretary for Education shuffled through his papers, as if he might find the answers there, like a joker in a pack of cards.

'You see, sir, we aren't sure how much this technology will cost in real terms, but we hope it will be less than we'd have to spend providing the same education by other means.'

'You really expect me to believe that these new machines can teach just as well as my teachers? Where's your proof? What's happened in other countries?'

'Well, sir, we certainly don't know much yet about what children learn this way, but there's a similar project starting in Bothana in 1980.'

The Minister frowned and said, in a snarling tone, 'So, we don't know what it costs and we don't know whether it works, but you still expect me to risk my political reputation on it. What's the alternative?'

'More and more children not being educated sir,' the Secretary said quietly.

'Why's that?'

'We can't afford the usual education any more, sir. We simply must try to increase our cost-effectiveness by using technology.'

'But can technology increase the cost-effectiveness of education?'

'There's some doubt if you will ever know whether

technology can increase education's cost-effectiveness,' inter-jected the Professor, unable to restrain himself any longer.

Across the table, the Minister looked even more annoyed. He really needed an answer.

'We haven't had great success in judging cost-effectiveness in education', the Professor went on, puffing on his pipe. 'Many of the assumptions underlying this type of analysis simply don't apply in the field of education. You can't treat education as an industry, for example.'

'But surely the chances of carrying out this analysis are increased when technology is introduced on a grand scale?', asked the Secretary.

'Well, the problems lie in identifying costs and effects and then in measuring them. We're getting better at it, but it isn't easy.'

'My members want to know how this new technology will improve their working conditions. They want the money to be spent on employing more teachers, to reduce class sizes. That would be the best way to increase their cost-effectiveness,' claimed the President of the Union of Teachers.

'Hmmm,' said the Minister, 'if we can't measure the cost-effectiveness of technology, we'll have even less chance of measuring the cost-effectiveness of that strategy.'
'You see what I mean', the President trumpeted, 'if you can't tell how cost-effective the teachers are, how can you com-pare them with the new educational media?'

Jean-Claude Eicher et al., 1982

PRE-1970S

Prior to 1970 the economics of distance teaching at university level in the west revolved mainly around the distance/external/ independent study departments of conventional universities. In the main, these departments were funded, as was conventional education, by government Ministries of Education from public monies, though the weighting for an external student was nor-mally lower than that of an on-campus student.

In many American universities, distance departments (even when students were studying for college credit) were grouped

Figure 10.1 Cost structures of proprietary distance systems

with continuing education departments and had to be self-supporting. Much of the rest of the world of distance education was proprietary in the early 1970s, if one excepts the correspondence schools and colleges of external studies run by the Australian state and Canadian provincial departments of education and the French CNTE (now CNED).

Prior to 1970 the cost equation for some proprietary distance education institutions seemed to be based on producing learning materials as cheaply as possible and then enrolling as many students as possible. There was little protective legislation at this period and the national accrediting agencies were not as influential as they were later to become.

There were, on the other hand, many excellent proprietary institutions in the 1970s and earlier – one thinks especially of the members of the US Distance Education and Training Council, formerly the National Home Study Council, the European Association of Correspondence Schools, and the British Association of Correspondence Colleges and similar accrediting associations. For these an analysis would combine the production of learning materials of quality with the costs of ensuring success for students enrolled (See Figure 10.1).

THE ECONOMICS OF THE OPEN UNIVERSITY (UK)

Cost analyses of the OUUK 1

Wagner (1972) provided the first cost analysis of a distance system with the entry of the OUUK into the field of distance education. He applied the cost structures of conventional universities (CU), taken largely from the Robbins Report, to the budgetary data of the OUUK. The results were impressively in favour of the OU:

- the average recurrent cost per equivalent undergraduate at the OU was only 25 per cent of that of CUs;
- the capital cost per student place at the OU was only 6 per cent of the conventional figure;
- the average recurrent cost per graduate – which depends on drop-outs – would be in favour of the OU unless its drop-out rate went over 85 per cent; and
- the resource cost per equivalent undergraduate at the OU was only 16 per cent of that of CUs.

Wagner accepted that the output, the OU graduate, would be similar to that of conventional universities although he admitted that there was a problem with research as OU academics did less. He costed the OU teaching package in five sections: correspondence materials, TV, radio programmes, classes at study centres, and residential summer schools. He regarded the course development components as fixed costs 'the expense of the impersonal components is in effect a fixed cost' (1972: 165) and the major variable cost 'is that concerned with the provision of personal tuition services' (1972: 167).

Wagner showed that in capital costs at the OU, student, cultural, recreational, library, and catering facilities do not have to be provided. He realized the central importance of drop-outs on average recurrent costs per student – if one designs a system for 50,000 students one may have a cost-effective system; however, if most drop out, one has a very costly system. However, even in 1972 Wagner refused to accept traditional drop-out statistics for correspondence schools as relevant to his cost structure for the OU. 'The OU is an innovation,' he wrote. 'The OU is much more than a correspondence college, since it offers an integrated system of teaching in which TV, radio, personal tuition and correspondence all play a part' (1972: 177).

Carter (1973) objected strongly, stating that a university exists to provide an educational experience, not just to turn out equivalent graduates and that Wagner was costing two quite different kinds of educational experience. Wagner, he said, had not costed CU facilities like medicine, nor was his allowance for research at

CUs adequate. OU courses were all low level; much of the costs of CUs were for laboratories for postgraduate students.

Carter also claimed that Wagner had forgotten to cost all the services that CUs were doing for the OU (residential schools, study centres, and libraries, etc.).

Wagner replied by recalculating his costs to include science and making adjustments for research, but did not accept most of Carter's other claims. The revised costings came out with little difference from his previous analysis because, Wagner said, Carter was confusing consumption and investment benefits (1973b: 72). In Wagner's view although the 'educational experience' of the community as measured by future earnings of OU graduates would be the same.

In a 1973 paper in *Universities Quarterly* Wagner represented his arguments in the context of a national goal of expanding the 15 per cent of each age cohort who entered higher education in the UK in 1971. He suggested the substitution of capital for labour by increasing the role of impersonal tuition by means of correspondence and broadcasting at the OU since 'educational technology remains at CUs a *complement* to existing methods of tuition instead of a *substitute*' (1973a: 404).

Wagner now admitted the validity of more of Carter's claims and re-presented his figures in slightly modified form. His general conclusion of the cost effectiveness of the OU was unchanged. 'Academic salaries', he states, 'which are the main item in costs at a conventional university take up less than 15 % of OUUK costs and are unrelated to student numbers' (1973a: 398). He also pointed out that the OUUK system was devised for its educational effectiveness as a distance teaching system, not because it was cheap (1973a: 400). Various ways of making it cheaper are considered: reducing personal tuition and increasing correspondence being the basic ones.

Cost analyses of the OUUK 2

Laidlaw and Layard (1974) moved the analysis from the cost of the OUUK to the costs of courses at the OUUK, seeking to throw light on the costs of OU teaching methods as against conventional 'live' instruction.

They distinguish between four 'types of cost' at the OU (1974: 445):

1 *fixed course costs*: inescapable if the course is put on;
2 *variable course costs*: costs which are dependent on student volume;
3 *fixed central costs*: inescapable if the OU is to exist; and
4 *variable central university costs*: which alter with the volume of students.

They conclude, like Wagner, that the real strength of the OU system is 'the potential economies of scale which can be replaced by substituting capital for labour' (1974: 452).

This means that a major part of the costs of the course become fixed and invariant with respect to student numbers. By contrast, campus universities' courses have low fixed costs but high marginal costs. For low levels of operation the campus university is the more efficient system and for high levels the OU is.

The break-even point in 1971 was calculated at 21,691 students, at which point the OUUK average cost per student would be lower than that for CUs.

Cost analyses of the OUUK 3

In 1975 Lumsden and Ritchie presented a survey and cost analysis of the OUUK. Their argument tends to support the position taken up by both Wagner and Laidlaw/Layard. In particular they attempt to answer the question 'What is the contribution towards the final degree of an average student year in the OU compared to an average student year in a conventional university?' and provide four different sets of answers. The article speaks of 'mass-media lectures' (1975: 238) on radio and television as central to the system and concludes with a discussion of the costing of a television university in the US.

Cost analyses fo the OUUK 4

In 1977 Wagner returned to the debate with a well-known article 'The economics of the OU revisited'. His appraisal of his forecasts of expenditure in the earlier articles was that they were generally accurate but that the OU had admitted more students then planned so that some costs were, in fact, marginally lower.

In this new study the input is weighted even more heavily in favour of the OU by claiming that costings should not be of graduates, but of what is value-added to produce the graduate. Thus in British CUs one starts with at least two 'A' levels; at the OU one starts normally with much less. No re-evaluation of output (the value of the graduate from OU or CU to employers, the community, or postgraduate research) is, however, considered necessary.

The 1977 article introduces data for forecast and more sophisticated analysis of distance systems. Thus, the drop-out rate of finally enrolled students is set at 25 per cent per course; the costs of course production are rightly assigned to the years before presentation (1977: 366); the equation $C = a + bx + cy$, where C = total costs; a = fixed costs; x = number of courses; y = number of students and b and c are the annual cost allocations per course and per student, is introduced from Laidlaw and Layard (1974) and Rumble (1976). A new distinction is made between new course production and maintenance of existing courses.

There are two major conclusions from Wagner's 1977 study: first, most of the economies of scale of the OU had been reaped within the first few years and there was little hope of further reductions. This was because the economies of increasing student numbers had been used by the OU to increase the number of courses in development and on offer rather than to reach the steady state, and because it proved impossible to improve academic productivity, especially for full-time tenured staff once the institutional patterns had gelled. Second, his analysis can offer little guidance on policy change within the OU or on the planning of other distance systems.

It is a little disappointing that Wagner offers no comparisons with other systems nor with variants on the OU system. Some suggestions are made (1977: 371), however, on reducing face-to-face tutoring, reducing summer school attendance, lowering the quality of printing or layout materials – the normal suggestions that distance systems face when they need to cut costs. Wagner claims that all of these would change the nature of the product the OU offers to students.

Carnoy and Levin (1975) and Mace (1978) were the first to challenge these conclusions. Carnoy and Levin claim that:

The limited nature of Open University education as well as the credential effect of particular institutions on earnings and occupational attainments would suggest that the Open University graduate is not likely to receive either consumption or income benefits from his education that are as high as those of the person from the more conventional university setting.

(Carnoy and Levin 1975: 391)

Mace considered that the claim of the OU to be more cost-effective than CUs was not substantiated. His OU article challenged both the economic analysis of Wagner and the 'openness' of the OU as it had been presented in a number of articles, especially by McIntosh (1976).

Mace's position is clear:

> It is concluded after an examination of the methodology and the evidence, that neither the economic case nor the social case is substantiated. Moreover, this view of the OU's performance may constitute a dangerous myth, because it may well inhibit further attempts at economic evaluation of the OU.

(Mace 1978: 295)

Mace bases much of his criticism of Wagner on the evaluation of the output of the OU system; earnings forgone, competitiveness on the labour market, and the value-added by the OU. He accepts Wagner's costing that it takes one-half of CU costs to produce a graduate at the OU and one-third of CU costs for the average recurrent annual cost per student, but asks whether the measure of output (graduates), could be produced more cheaply by reducing or reallocating resources between the various items in the OU budget (1978: 305).

The answer is that it could but that you produce a different teaching package and this alters the quality and possibly the quantity of the output. Mace's main candidates for reduction are television broadcasting and class tutorials which, he suggests, could be reduced without affecting the quantity, quality, and status of the output.

COST ANALYSES OF DISTANCE SYSTEMS

The economics of distance systems takes on a new dimension with the chapter by Neil *et al.* in the 1979 book *Fernstudien an*

Universitäten edited by Dörfler and published in Vienna. It is clear from the opening sentence that the parochialism of the Wagner–Mace debate has been left behind:

> In numerous instances, we have observed the launching of distance learning systems for which the fundamental variables which affect costs to a significant extent have either not been made explicit or have not been given explicit working values in initial budgeting exercises.
>
> (Neil *et al.* 1979: 3)

Valuable as the economic analyses of the OU had been, they had not extrapolated from the context of a single institution which has been described as *sui generis* (Daniel and Stroud 1981: 148) and which offers an unusual, if highly successful, costing mix of extensive television broadcasting with large amounts of compulsory and optional face-to-face sessions – a costing structure characteristic of none of the five models in this book's typology, not even Group 2: the distance teaching universities.

Neil *et al.* base themselves on the economic analyses of distance teaching systems outlined above *plus* the work done on the economic analysis of media in education during the 1970s by Eicher, Jamison, Kleès, Wells, and others. As a result they seek to provide costing processes that will be of value to all workers in distance systems.

They express the cost functions so far established as:

$$TC = F + VN$$

where TC = total costs; F = fixed costs; V = variable cost per unit of output (N); and N = number of units of output (students/ student hours, etc.). When the total cost function is linear, the average cost (AC) is simply equal to the fixed cost dividend by N plus the variable cost (V), so that AC = F/N + V and the marginal cost is equal to V.

They confirm the findings of previous studies, especially those of Laidlaw and Layard:

- The cost structures of distance learning systems differ significantly from those of traditional instructional systems (1979: 98).
- Distance systems have high fixed costs and low variable costs

relative to conventional campus-based universities (Laidlaw and Layard 1974).

- Distance systems have potential for effecting economies of scale: as the number of students increases so the average cost declines by spreading the fixed cost over more units (1979: 98).
- For smaller numbers of students, campus-based universities using traditional instructions are more efficient, but for higher numbers a distance system is more efficient (1979: 100).
- Design and production costs are generally much higher than the costs of transmission and reception (1979: 100).
- There must be sufficient students to allow economies of scale to be reaped (1979: 102).

The authors then present their own financial model of a distance system based on three major areas of costing: (1) the organization, (2) the number of courses, and (3) the number of students.

This study is important because it transformed what had been a series of studies of a particular institution into a modelling process for distance systems in general; it used the work of Eicher, Jamison, and others on the costing of educational communications media, and it separated clearly the analysis of cost-inducing variables in distance education systems from the economics of conventional insititutions.

CANADIAN SMALL DISTANCE EDUCATION SYSTEMS

North American financial and management practice was brought into the economics of distance education as a result of studies at Athabasca University, Edmonton, Alberta by Snowden and Daniel. They present (1980: 78) a cost equation for small distance education systems based on the two functions of course development and services by delivery:

$$TC = a_1 (x_1 + x_2/l) + by + c$$

where

x_1 = course credits 'in development';
x_2 = course credits 'in delivery';
l = the lifetime of a course in delivery, where it is assumed that the total cost of maintenance over the life of a course is equal

172

to that of developing a course; l is taken to be five years in practice;

y = weighted course enrolments. Course enrolments are on the basis of a standard six-credit course, such that a student enrolled on a three-credit course is equal to 0.5 of a standard course enrolment;

a_1 = course development costs per credit;

b = delivery costs per weighted course enrolment; and

c = costs of institutional overheads.

This model differentiates costs for courses in development which will be taught in the future from courses already developed which are now being taught.

Snowden and Daniel show that the average recurrent cost per course enrolment declines as the number of course enrolments increases, but at a declining rate, so that once a small distance education system reaches about 10,000 course enrolments, with a media mix and student support services similar to those of Athabasca University, then futher economies of scale cannot be expected to be important.

COSTING OF EDUCATIONAL TECHNOLOGY

The economics of new educational media have been studied by a number of leading experts in the field of the use of new communications technology in education: J.-C. Eicher, D.T. Jamison, S. Klees, E. McAnany, J. Mayo, F. Orivel, H. Perraton, and P. Suppes. Schramm's 1977 overview *Big Media Little Media* is also well known. These studies have been summarized in a three-volume UNESCO study (Eicher *et al.* 1977, 1980, 1982) and in a volume edited for the World Bank by Perraton (1982a).

These studies deal with the costing of the use of certain new communications media in education and not with whole distance education systems costs. Many of the programmes which are central to the economic analyses of these studies would not be included in the definition of distance education adopted for this book. For a true costing of such projects one would have to include the school buildings, other plant, and some of the payment to the face-to-face teachers. This would confuse the functional basis for the economics of distance systems.

In 1982 Perraton published *The Cost of Distance Education*, a

173

65-page summary of the evidence to date analysing the Wagner, Laidlaw–Layard, Snowden–Daniel, Rumble series of studies, together with the work of Eicher, Jamison and the UNESCO/ World Bank series, and providing his own synthesis (1982b).

WHOLE DISTANCE EDUCATION SYSTEM COSTS

Rumble had established his cost analysis and financial modelling structures by the late 1970s. In the early 1980s he set about applying his structures to actual situations. This produced two major economic case-studies of UNED in Costa Rica (1981a: 375–401) and of UNA in Venezuela (1982: 116–40) and an overview of economics and cost structures which was published as chapter 12 of *Distance Teaching for Higher and Adult Education* (1981b: 220–34).

In his 1982 article Rumble presented a 'state of the art' analysis of the economics of distance education as it was in 1980. The presentation is so nuanced, qualified, and comprehensive that it is best to present here his conclusions almost in full:

- Broadly speaking, very significant costs are incurred in the preparation of materials irrespective of student numbers. The level of cost incurred will vary depending on the choice of media. Production costs of television are high but not as high as for film. The production cost of radio is relatively low. Print production costs vary depending on the level of sophistication, but overall are not normally significant in themselves within the context of a particular project. Where print is the principal medium the cost of academic staff time in its design and development may be significant.

- Transmission and duplication costs are very high for video systems. The cost of film and of video-cassette based systems increases with the magnitude of the project. The cost of distributing print and audio-visual materials to students depends on the means of distribution used, population dispersal, and difficulty of access to the target population.

- In conventional educational systems teaching costs are traditionally held to be a recurrent cost that is variable with the number of students in the system. In contrast, in distance learning systems the cost of developing the materials can be regarded as a fixed cost that can be written off over the life of the course of which they form a part. This investment has been seen as analogous to capital investment in business, representing a move away from the labour intensive nature of conventional teaching systems. It follows that the more students there are using the materials, the lower the average cost per student of the materials. Hence at some point, and this depends on the choice of media, a distance teaching system should become cheaper per unit of output than a traditional system.

- The use of face-to-face tuition tends to undermine the cost advantage of distance teaching by re-introducing a cost element that is directly variable with student numbers. As a result, face-to-face contact is usually restricted particularly at the higher level and has a different function to that found in conventional systems, where it is a major teaching medium.
- From an economic point of view the investment in course materials is not normally warranted where student numbers are small. As a result the choice of courses in distance teaching systems may be restricted, at least in comparison with conventional systems.
- Administrative systems for the control of course design, production and distribution and for the teaching of students at a distance tend to be more clearly differentiated from the academic functions than is the case in conventional systems, as well as being more complex in themselves. The initial investment in administrative systems prior to the enrolment of any students is likely to be significant and on the whole more costly than is the case in conventional systems.

(Rumble 1982: 119–20)

Rumble's work in a number of distance systems enabled him to identify the main generators of costs in a distance system and to show how the costs change as key input or output variables change.

COSTING OF DISTANCE TEACHING UNIVERSITIES

Keegan and Rumble (1982) applied these economic analyses to the distance teaching universities. Distance teaching universities (DTUs), they conclude, can be cost effective in comparison with conventional universities, but this may not necessarily be the case. The cost advantage of distance teaching universities can be undermined if (1982: 220):

- the investment in media and materials is excessive, relative to the number of students in the system;
- the direct student costs (or variable cost per student) is above or on a par with those at conventional universities – in which case the DTU will *never* achieve economies of scale relative to conventional universities;
- the variable cost per student in a DTU is only marginally lower than that in a coventional university, since in this case the DTU will need proportionally more students if its average costs are to drop significantly below that of the conventional universities; or
- the DTU cannot attract sufficient students to warrant the investment in the development of its materials and systems.

These factors have important implications for the provision of face-to-face tuition. The more face-to-face tuition is built into a distance teaching system, the nearer variable student costs will be to those found in conventional universities.

Yet if one considers that the quality of academic provision makes an extensive face-to-face element essential in a distance teaching university, then DTUs with relatively low student numbers may not be able both to improve the quality of their provision and retain their present level of cost efficiency relative to conventional universities in their country or province.

COSTING OF AUTONOMOUS AND MIXED DISTANCE INSTITUTIONS

In their 1982 study Keegan and Rumble then proceeded with an attempt to compare the cost structures of autonomous distance teaching institutions (Groups 1 and 2) with the distance departments of conventional institutions (Groups 3–5). They came up with the following cost indicators:

- once an annual minimum of enrolments is guaranteed for the distance system some indicators favour the distance system being autonomous;
- the costs associated with establishing an infrastructure for a distance system and the cost of the preparation of initial course materials are such that a mixed system is to be preferred if an annual minimum of enrolments cannot be guaranteed;
- the annual minimum number of enrolments probably lies in the region 9,000–20,000; and
- these financial indicators depend always on the choice of media, the extent of student support services, the number of courses on offer, and the costs of conventional education in the country.

CONCLUSION

From an analysis of all the studies presented in this chapter certain economic indicators on the costing of distance systems can be put together:

- The economics of conventional education is of little value for the cost analysis of distance systems.
- The equation frequently used in conventional education as the basis for system costs:

$$\text{Faculty salary expense} = \frac{\text{Weekly student hours} \times \text{average faculty salary}}{\text{Average class size} \times \text{average faculty load}}$$

has little relevance in distance education.

- The proportion of fixed costs to total costs in conventional education (schools, colleges, and universities) is small; this is not true of distance systems.
- Distance systems, like industries, have high capital investment in the production of courses; conventional education is labour-intensive.
- The number of drop-outs in the system is crucial; once drop-outs pass 50 per cent and move towards 100 per cent cost effectiveness vanishes.
- If student support services are face to face and compulsory,

cost structures rapidly return towards those of conventional education. Some authors appear to suggest that academic success or reduction of drop-out may be linked to provision of student services.

Within these caveats it is clear that there is now available a comprehensive costing system for distance education.

APPLICATION

An attempt is now made to apply these conclusions to the costing of a hypothetical distance system.

We know from studies by Wagner and Laidlaw–Layard on the OUUK, by Snowden and Daniel on Athabasca University, and by Rumble on a series of DTUs, that costs of a distance teaching system have the following characteristics:

- high fixed costs;
- low variable costs per student;
- design and production costs of materials which depend on the choice of media.

We know that the variable costs per student are dependent on the following variables:

- number of local centres;
- number of courses in production;
- number of students.

In acordance with this analysis it is possible to develop a mathematical cost function for a distance education system.

The cost of the system in any year is:

$$T + Z$$

where T = recurrent costs and Z = fixed costs (plant, buildings), because

$$T = F + L\alpha + D\beta + C\gamma + Sx$$

where T = recurrent costs; F = recurrent fixed costs; L = number of local centres; α = average cost of a local centre; D = number of courses in production, β = cost of design and production of a course; C = number of courses in presentation; γ = average cost of presentation of a course; S = number of students; and x = average cost per student.

Let us hypothesize that there are six local centres (L), thirteen courses in development (D), eleven courses in presentation (C), and 500 students (S), and that costs are calculated as follows:

Plant and buildings	$850,000
Fixed recurrent costs	$2,031,200
Average cost of a local centre	$26,073
Average cost of producing a course	$12,033
Average cost of presenting a course	$18,454
Average cost per student	$829

In accordance with these data the costs of the system for a full year are:

Fixed costs (Z)=	$850,000
Recurrent costs (T)=	$2,961,561

Recurrent cost are made up of:

F =	$2,031,200
$L\alpha = \$26{,}073 \times 6$ =	$156,438
$D\beta = \$12{,}033 \times 13$ =	$156,429
$C\gamma = \$18{,}454 \times 11$ =	$202,994
$Sx = \$829 \times 500$ =	$414,500
Total	$2,961,561

Thus total system costs ($Z+T$) are $3,811,561 and total annual costs (T) are $2,961,561.

DIFFERING LEVELS OF ACTIVITY

In addition one can analyse the costs of a system if it has an increased level of activity. For example let us assume that there are now:

- 8 local centres;
- 60 courses in presentation;
- 10 courses that are remade each year or that each course is remade once every 6 years or that 10 courses are produced each year; and
- 500 or 1,000 or 5,000, or 10,000, or 20,000 students.

Then the total cost (*T*) is:

Fixed	$2,031,200
8 local centres	$208,584
60 courses in presentation	$1,107,240
10 courses in production	$120,330

and there are

500 students	$414,500
1,000 students	$829,000
5,000 students	$4,145,000
10,000 students	$8,290,000
20,000 students	$16,580,000

Therefore total system costs for different student levels are:

Number	Total costs	Average cost per student
500	$3,881,854	$7,763 p.a.
1,000	$4,296,354	$4,296 p.a.
5,000	$7,612,354	$1,522 p.a.
10,000	$11,757,354	$1,176 p.a.
20,000	$20,047,354	$1,002 p.a.

COMPARATIVE COSTS

Finally, Rumble has provided us with graphs for demonstrating the comparative costs of distance and conventional students.

Assuming that a certain distance system has fixed costs which are three times those of a conventional system, and that its variable costs are one-third of those of a conventional system, then at a certain point the distance system becomes cheaper per capita than the conventional system. Figure 10.2 (Rumble 1981b: 222) shows that fixed costs are constant for campus-based and distance learning systems and are always higher for the distance system. Variable costs, on the other hand, start lower for the campus-based system but quickly reach a break-even point, from which stage on costs are always higher for the conventional system.

When student numbers and unit costs are compared in conventional and distance learning systems (Rumble 1981b: 233) as in Figure 10.3 it is seen that the cost curve quickly favours the distance system but that as student numbers annually increase

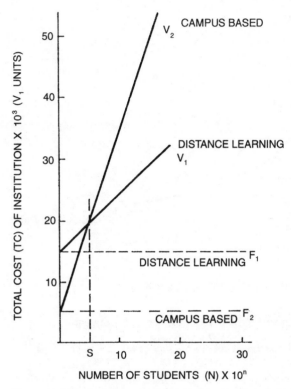

Figure 10.2 The cost structure of conventional and distance education
systems
Source: Reproduced with permission from Kaye and Rumble (1981)

beyond the 30,000 mark, the curve tends to flatten out and
remains permanently parallel to and significantly below the
costs of a conventional system.

FURTHER ANALYSES

Rumble addressed the question of when a distance system is
more costly than a conventional system and when it can be

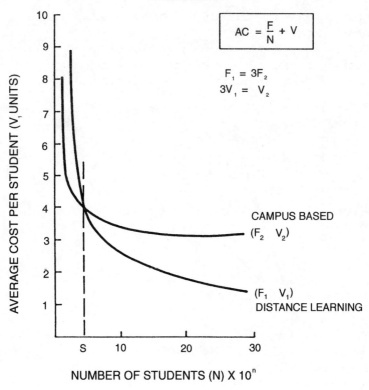

$$AC = \frac{F}{N} + V$$

$$F_1 = 3F_2$$
$$3V_1 = V_2$$

Figure 10.3 Student numbers and unit costs in conventional and
distance systems
Source: Reproduced with permission from Kaye and Rumble (1981)

cheaper in an article published in 1987. Using data from Laidlaw
and Layard and from his earlier publications he compared the
cost structures of a first year Arts course and a second year
Geography course at the Open University of the UK and at a
contemporary British university. His conclusions show clearly
that some courses at a distance can be cheaper and some can be
dearer depending on the cost-inducing variables:

The fixed costs of the first Arts Foundation course offered by
the Open University (OU) was £162,558. A comparable
course in a conventional university (CU) had fixed costs of
£401, a CU to OU ratio of 1:405. The variable costs of the OU
course were £56 as compared with £117, an OU to CU ratio

182

of about 1:2. The ratio of variable fixed costs in a CU was 1:3.4. In the OU it was 1:2903. The Open University course had to have 2658 students on it in order to have an average cost equivalent to that of a conventional university course.

Another OU course, on geography (D281), had a fixed cost of £73,702 compared with a CU fixed cost of £671. Its variable cost was £109, while the comparable variable costs in CUs was only £87. Here, the OU course could never be more cost-efficient than the CU's equivalent offerings.

Yet another OU course (S22-) in science, had a fixed cost of £95,007 against a CU cost of £666. Its variable cost of £100 was lower than the CU equivalent of £218. Hence it needed a student population of 800 to have average student costs equivalent to that of a CU course. In fact, it only achieved this once in its life, so, while potentially the OU could have reaped the benefits of economies of scale on this course, it did not because it had insufficient students to do so.

(Rumble 1987: 76)

In 1986 Rumble provided a monograph *Activity Costing in Mixed-Mode Institutions* as a guide to Group 5 institutions (the Australian integrated mode) and in 1987 Markowitz published a study of Group 3 institutions (independent study departments) under the title 'Financial decision making – calculating the cost of distance education'.

In the 1990s the introduction of synchronous technologies into distance systems brought about a swing of system costs back towards the economics of conventional systems for distance systems in which synchronous technologies are used. In two-way video, two-way audio codec systems or in two-way audio, one-way video satellite systems, the institution has to build or hire electronic classrooms for the grouping of students. Students, in their turn, have to pay for travel to attend the group meetings. Substantial modifications are introduced to the characteristic features of the economics of distance systems: high start-up costs; economies of scope; economies of scale; costs amortized over the shelf-life of courses; variable costs per student often calculated on no or optional student groupings.

REFERENCES

Carnoy, M. and Levin, H. (1975) 'Evaluation of educational media: some issues', *Instructional Science* 4, 385–406.

Carter, C.F. (1973) 'The economics of the OU: a comment', *Higher Education* 1, 285–8.

Daniel, J. and Stroud, M. (1981) 'Distance education – a reappraisal for the 1980s', *Distance Education* 2(2), 146–63.

Eicher, J.-C. *et al.* (1977, 1980, 1982) *The Economics of New Educational Media*, Paris: UNESCO.

Kaye, A. and Rumble, G. (eds) (1981) *Distance Education for Higher and Adult Education*, London: Croom Helm.

Keegan, D. and Rumble, G. (1982) 'Characteristics of the distance teaching universities', in G. Rumble and K. Harry (eds) *The Distance Teaching Universities*, London: Croom Helm.

Laidlaw, B. and Layard, R. (1974) 'Traditional versus OU teaching methods: a cost comparison', *Higher Education* 3, 439–68.

Lumsden, K. and Ritchie, C. (1975) 'The Open University: a survey and cost analysis', *Instructional Science* 4, 237–61.

Mace, J. (1978) 'Mythology in the making: is the OU really cost effective?', *Higher Education* 7, 295–309.

McIntosh, N. (1976) *A Degree of Difference*, Guildford: SRHE.

Markowitz, H. (1987) 'Financial decision making – calculating the costs of distance education', *Distance Education* 8(2), 147–60.

Neil, M., Rumble, G. and Tout, A. (1979) 'Some aspects of modelling for recurrent cost budgeting and forecasting in distance learning systems', in W. Dörfert (ed.) *Fernstudien an Universitäten*, Klagenfurt: UVD.

Perraton, H. (1982a) *Alternative Routes to Formal Education*, Washington: World Bank.

Perraton, H. (1982b) *The Cost of Distance Education*, Cambridge: IEC.

Rumble, G. (1976) 'Management and costing models for distance teaching', in J. Hakemulder, (ed.) *Distance Education for Development*, Bonn: German Foundation for International Development.

Rumble, G. (1981a) 'The cost analysis of distance teaching: Costa Rica's UNED', *Higher Education* 10, 375–401

Rumble, G. (1981b) 'Economics and cost structures', in A. Kaye and G. Rumble (eds) *Distance Teaching for Higher and Adult Education*, London: Croom Helm.

Rumble, G. (1982) 'The cost analysis of learning at a distance. Venezuela's UNA', *Distance Education* 3(1), 116–40.

Rumble, G. (1986) *Activity Costing in Mixed-Mode Institutions*, Geelong: Deakin University.

Rumble, G. (1987) 'Why distance education can be cheaper than conventional education', *Distance Education* 8(1), 72–94.

Schramm, W. (1977) *Big Media, Little Media*, London: Sage.

Snowden, B. and Daniel, J. (1980) 'The economics and management of small, post-secondary distance education systems', *Distance Education* 1(1), 68–91.

Wagner, L. (1972) 'The econimics of the Open University', *Higher Education*, 2, 159–83.

Wagner, L. (1973a) 'The OU and the costs of expanding higher education', *Universities Quarterly* 390–410.

Wagner, L (1973b) 'The economics of the OU: a reply', *Higher Education*, 3, 21–7.

Wagner, L. (1977) 'The economics of the OU revisted', *Higher Education* 6, 359–81.

11

APPRAISAL OF SELECTED SYSTEMS

'I've taught the dog to whistle.'
'I can't hear it whistling.'
'I didn't say it had learned to whistle.'

From a cartoon strip, 1977

In their appraisal of the success or failure of the distance teaching universities (DTUs) Keegan and Rumble (1982) used a four-point evaluation scheme of their effectiveness. This evaluation plan is recommended here as suitable for the overall evaluation of any distance teaching system. Evaluation is focused on:

- the quantity of the learning achieved;
- the quality of the learning achieved;
- the status of the learning achieved;
- the relative cost of the learning achieved.

THE QUANTITY OF THE LEARNING ACHIEVED

Under this heading are considered:

- the success of the system in widening access, not just in terms of absolute numbers but also in attracting specific target groups;
- drop-outs;
- the quantity of the output relative to the input (the output/input ratio);
- the time it takes to produce the output; and
- the system's success in satisfying national, local and individual needs.

To receive a satisfactory evaluation the institution is required

186

to achieve measurable success in (1) the avoidance of avoidable drop-out; (2) the number of successful students as a proportion of the number of students admitted; (3) the time it takes for students to achieve successful outcomes.

THE QUALITY OF LEARNING ACHIEVED

Under this heading is grouped the gathering of data for the evaluation of:

- the quality of the learning materials provided by the distance system;
- the extent to which distance teaching is a suitable vehicle for educating students in certain subjects;
- the extent to which education is provided, as opposed to instruction;
- the effectiveness of learning at a distance;
- the 'intersubjectivity' of learning at a distance.

THE STATUS OF THE LEARNING ACHIEVED

Indications of the status accorded the learning achieved by distance students come from:

- the extent to which other educational institutions recognize the studies for credit transfer purposes;
- the acceptance of the degrees and diplomas awarded as qualifying students to go on to higher level studies;
- the recognition of the awards by employers; and
- the esteem in which the distance teaching institutions and their awards are held in the community at large.

The status of distance programmes can be measured and data collected for evaluation on the extent to which other educational institutions recognize the studies for credit transfer; the acceptance of the distance degrees for higher level studies; and the recognition of the awards by managers in competitive interviews for employment.

THE RELATIVE COST OF THE LEARNING ACHIEVED

Keegan and Rumble were concerned here with:

- the cost-efficiency of distance universities relative to conventional universities or to other modes of internal operation which the distance universities could adopt;
- the cost-effectiveness of distance universities relative to conventional universities – the concept of cost-effectiveness tries to weigh the relative value of the outputs in qualitative terms;
- the cost benefits of distance and traditional university education, in which the costs of the education provided and the benefits (direct and indirect, financial and social) to the individual and society are taken into account: and
- the opportunity cost of education at a distance.

It has been said that teaching at a distance should cost more than conventional education; things at a distance usually do. However, the history of proprietary correspondence schools had shown the way to mass education by demonstrating how large numbers of students could be enrolled in distance programmes at a low average cost, once the initial capital outlay in the development of learning materials had been undertaken. Studies by Wagner and others showed that similar patterns were achievable by government-sponsored distance teaching institutions.

CASE-STUDIES

Five institutions are evaluated in accordance with the criteria listed. One institution has been chosen from each of the groupings in the typology of chapter 8. The Centre National d'Enseignement à Distance in France represents the schools and colleges of Group 1, and the Chinese Radio and TV University Network represents the open universities of Group 2. Groups 3 to 5 are represented by the Department of Independent Study at the University of Florida in the United States, Contact North/ Nord in Canada and the Australian Distance Education Centre at the University of New England respectively.

To reflect the diversity and complexity of distance education world-wide, the institutions have been chosen from differing national education systems, and they have different assessment procedures and ideological frameworks. Two of the institutions work normally in English, one in French, one in Chinese and one in English and French. In addition to providing an appraisal of the differing systems the aim has been to give the reader a pen-picture of the day-to-day working of the systems. Even in the late 1990s there is still considerable lack of knowledge among students of distance education on how the Chinese system works or how an American university department of independent studies carries out its functions.

GROUP 1: CENTRE NATIONAL D'ENSEIGNEMENT À DISTANCE (CNED) (NATIONAL CENTRE FOR DISTANCE TEACHING, FRANCE)

Institution

The central administration of the CNED is at Asterama II, 86980 Futuroscope Cedex, Poitiers, France. Telephone: 003349–499494. The invasion of France led to the creation of the Centre National d'Enseignement par Correspondance (CNEC) by a government decree of 2 December 1939 to meet the needs of schoolchildren dislocated by war. In the mid-1980s the name was changed to its present form, CNED, which might be translated as National Centre for Distance Teaching.

Structure

The CNED is a public administrative establishment under the supervision of the French Ministry of Education, comprising a central directorate and eight institutes. When the annual enrolment in Paris reached 150,000 in the early 1970s a major structural change was achieved. Administrative control of programmes was divided into six centres: Paris (Vanves), Grenoble, Lille, Lyon, Rouen and Toulouse. Rennes was added in 1982 and the eighth, Poitiers-Futuroscope, in 1992. A decree of 7 May 1988 restructured the governing body of the CNED (Conseil d'Administration) to comprise representatives of industry, politics, and the universities. A protocol of 30 March 1988 on university distance education in France brought the CNED into contact with French university structures.

189

Staffing

The CNED model is that each of the eight centres is staffed by full-time staff who are specialists in distance education. Their time is divided between developing or revising courses for future students and teaching students at present enrolled in courses previously developed. The 2,750 courses are divided between the eight centres and are only available from that centre.

In 1995 the CNED had 6,939 staff. The full-time tenured staff of 1,800 are all employed by the Ministry of Education on the same terms as teachers in French schools, and there are 3,000 full-time academic staff on contracts. Eight hundred are employed in student contact and services, 400 in printing and publishing and there are 937 administrative staff. Of the teaching staff some have been assigned to the CNED because of physical or psychological disabilities and could not be transferred back to the face-to-face system. Many of the staff work full-time from their own homes, thus saving enormously on plant and buildings.

Students and courses

Each year in the 1990s the enrolment in the CNED has increased rapidly from a quarter of a million annually at the start of the decade to 350,000 in 1995 (see Table 11.1). The students come

Table 11.1 Annual enrolment at the Centre National d'Enseignement à Distance

Year	Student enrolments
1940	War years
1945	1,413
1950	8,300
1955	30,000
1960	61,000
1965	109,000
1970	146,000
1975	180,000
1980	197,000
1985	225,000
1990	250,000
1995	350,000

Source: Renseignements statistiques du CNED.

from nearly every country in the world. Of the 1995 enrolment 15 per cent represents the original mandate of primary and secondary schooling at a distance. Access is provided throughout the world, as it is traditional for French government and business officials, who are on assignment overseas, to enrol their children in the full French school programme at the CNED for the years in which the family is outside France.

Adults make up 85 per cent of the students and are enrolled in every level from post-literacy and numeracy to the equivalent of postgraduate university level courses (see Table 11.2).

Success and quantity of provision

For students in compulsory education aged 6–16 drop-out is not a phenomenon. Students pass easily from classroom education to correspondence and back. Those students resident in France receive a two-hour visit from a CNED teacher to their house (or hospital etc.) once a week. Students overseas receive comprehensive correspondence tuition from a personal tutor-counsellor assigned to them.

For an analysis of success and of drop-outs at the CNED the researcher can establish from government statistics the number of candidates (*étudiants admissibles*) who studied at the CNED and the number who studied face to face in ordinary institutions. When the results are published the researcher can establish the number and percentage of successful students who studied at a distance and the number and percentage of successful (*étudiants reçus*) students who studied face to face.

The CNED reports very creditable results in national competitive examinations, with results in humanities subjects being somewhat better than results in sciences and technology.

Quality of provision and status

The status of the qualification is guaranteed by the government in the same national competitive examinations as ordinary students take and employment is guaranteed for the graduates of the distance system if they are successful in winning a place in the quota of successful candidates.

CNED printed materials are functional. An A4 portrait format with a typeface that gives an average of twenty-two words per line and over forty lines per page gives a density of presentation that is relieved only rarely by line drawings. Margins are minimal (average 1.5 cm on both sides) and the use of headings, and other deictic devices is sparse.

On the other hand the quality of CNED's audio materials is excellent and tapes at all levels, and in languages as diverse as Russian and Chinese, make up an audio component of extensive quantity and quality.

Course development

Course development is by the individual full-time staff member, usually in consultation with colleagues in the same discipline. The materials are edited, commented upon, and approved by the head of department and sent to the production department for development. Extensive use is made of audio materials in music and language courses, in addition to slide packs, videocassettes and floppy discs.

Administrative responsibility for the development and remaking of the CNED's 2,750 courses is divided between the eight institutes (see Table 11.2)

Student support services

The main teaching strategies of the CNED for preparing its students for the national French examinations, once the audio and printed materials have been distributed, are correspondence tuition from a tutor-counsellor, often a full-time staff member, and occasional, voluntary face-to-face sessions.

In recent years increased use is being made of Minitel, telephone contacts, meetings and videotransmissions.

Costs

The CNED provides full-time staffing for the authorship of distance teaching materials, for the design and production of the materials and for student support services, with each student being linked to a personal tutor-counsellor at least for the length of one course. Thus most of the CNED budget goes on full-time staff. In 1993 this was over FF551 million.

Economies are made in contrast to other systems by the

Table 11.2 Distribution of programmes between the CNED centres

Centre	Programme
Grenoble	Industrial certificates Sport and Tourism Physical education Public service qualifications
Lille	Public service qualifications Law
Lyon	Accountancy Nursing Health education Commercial qualifications
Poitiers-Futuroscope	Industrial and services sectors Modern languages
Rennes	Paramedical qualifications Biotechnology Secondary education
Rouen	Communication and publicity Architecture Pharmacy
Toulouse	Primary education Teacher education Biological qualifications
Vanves (Paris)	DEUG (two-year university degree) Licence and diploma (university) Capes (teacher education) Capet (teacher education) *Agrégation*

Source: Renseignements statistiques du CNED

availability of full-time teaching staff to work on courses at various levels in the same discipline and from the use of the same production staff for the development of courses in all sectors.

The media mix is conservative with print dominating the learning materials, and correspondence, audiocassettes, and telephone being the main forms of support. In some parts of the system further economies are achieved as offices are provided only for senior staff with many staff working full-time from home.

In 1995 the annual enrolment fee per course was between FF1,000 and FF1,500.

GROUP 2: CHINESE RADIO AND TELEVISION UNIVERSITY NETWORK (DIANDA)

Institution

The Central Chinese Radio and Television University system is a network of forty-three provincial open or radio and television universities and one central university in Beijing. It was set up in 1979 to meet the urgent demands for skilled manpower and for adult education which the conventional system could not satisfy. The address of the Central Radio and TV University is 160 Fuxing Men Nei Street, Beijing 100031, P.R. China. Telephone 008610–6039048.

Structure

The Central Radio and TV University does not enrol any students but has responsibility for nation-wide course and materials development; the forty-three open universities enrol students but have a limited role in course and materials development.

The network of China's Radio and TV universities is organized at central and regional levels and has a five-tier structure made up of the Central Radio and TV University at the top, forty-three radio and TV universities at provincial level, 690 TV regional colleges at prefecture and city level, 1,600 TV education centres at county level and more than 10,000 tutorial groups, for the organization and operation of the whole system. Each level is directed and sponsored by the corresponding government educational authority in terms of annual budget appropriation, personnel appointments, policy-making and overall planning.

Staffing

The total number of full-time staff within the network is 43,000, of whom 18,000 are academic staff. The system also employs 13,000 part-time staff recruited from conventional institutions, adult education colleges, teacher-training colleges, business,

Table 11.3 Staffing and student statistics for the Chinese Radio and TV University network

Name of university	Staffing	Students
1 CRTVU	598	0
2 Beijing Open University	605	14,657
3 Tianjin Open University	1,285	21,562
4 Hebei Open University	1,807	24,791
5 Shanxi Open University	560	13,439
6 Inner Mongolian Open University	960	5,295
7 Liaoning Open University	1,392	46,965
8 Shenyang Open University	349	10,277
9 Dalian Open University	187	26,155
10 Jilin Open University	780	41,104
11 Changchun Open University	135	6,084
12 Heilongjiang Open University	2,302	30,529
13 Harbin Open University	399	6,341
14 Shanghai Open University	1,228	13,968
15 Jiangsu Open University	2,965	35,092
16 Nanjing Open University	625	4,494
17 Zhejiang Open University	1,172	35,352
18 Ningbo Open University	167	10,898
19 Anhui Open University	656	12,519
20 Fujian Open University	678	17,304
21 Xiamen Open University	62	2,373
22 Jiangxi Open University	801	13,088
23 Shandong Open University	3,734	40,037
24 Qingdao Open University	382	18,604
25 Henan Open University	2,188	41,673
26 Hubei Open University	2,239	22,297
27 Wuhan Open University	910	2,697
28 Hunan Open University	993	25,244
29 Guangdong Open University	1,950	34,015
30 Guangzhou Open University	223	6,562
31 Shenzhen Open University	134	3,489
32 Guangxi Open University	742	12,447
33 Hainan Open University	96	1,266
34 Sichuan Open University	1,083	34,176
35 Chengdu Open University	82	22,788
36 Chongqing Open University	136	10,483
37 Guizhou Open University	948	9,474
38 Yunnan Open University	570	37,392
39 Shaanxi Open University	1,622	10,181
40 Xian Open University	421	5,357
41 Gansu Open University	595	8,681
42 Qinghai Open University	86	613
43 Ningxia Open University	293	5,651
44 Xinjiang Open University	1,122	6,471
Total	40,262	751,885

Source: Education Statistics Yearbook of Radio and TV University in China.

public services or even high schools for the roles of TV programme presenters, textbook compilers, guest speakers on radio programmes as well as tutors for the face-to-face tutorials. The number of part-time faculty is usually decided by the annual enrolment, and generally the ratio between full-time and part-time staff is 1:1.

Table 11.3 shows the relationship between full-time staff and annual enrolment for 1995.

Students and courses

The student body is made up of in-service adults and high school graduates, of whom working adults represent 70 per cent of the total enrolment. The total number of students engaged in diploma programmes from 1979 to 1994 who have now graduated is 1.778 million. The latest statistics show a population of 3.46 million participating in non-degree programmes provided by the system.

The latest tracer survey in 1991 on degree higher education graduates showed that male students were 72 per cent of the student population. The average age was 24, with the oldest student enrolled 53 and the youngest 15 years of age. High school graduates are all required to study full-time, while in-service adults can study part-time or full-time based on the amount of study leave granted by their employers.

Success and quantity of provision

The system offers both degree and non-degree programmes. Degree courses are three- or two-year programmes, with the three-year courses being for full-time students majoring in engineering and technology; the two-year programmes are for full-time students of humanities and social sciences. Part-time students majoring in these two programmes are expected to finish their courses in from three to six years. The standard expected is that of the three-year Chinese diploma rather than the four-year Chinese bachelor degree.

Non-degree programmes are offered to serve the needs of short-term training, upgrading and updating of working adults in five sectors:

- in-service specialized training for job qualification;
- professional certification training for those with more than five years' working experience;
- continuing education for those who have already obtained a degree for the purpose of updating and upgrading;
- pre-job technical training for future members of the labour force;
- public education at various levels to improve the quality of the whole nation.

The system provides more than 350 courses in twenty-one disciplines for five degree programmes, and forty-eight courses in eighty-nine subjects in the non-degree programme.

Quality of provision and status

All the students reading for degree courses are required to take either the national entrance examination for traditional colleges and universities or the national entrance examination for adult education.

The majority of the textbook compilers, presenters and guest speakers on radio and TV programmes are well-known professors from conventional colleges and universities. Compulsory face-to-face tutorials are arranged for both full-time and part-time students. The ratio between radio/TV programmes and tutorials is 2:1, with the possibility of 1:1 or 3:1 in certain courses.

Student performance and progress throughout the course is assessed and measured by end-of-semester examinations at a fixed time on a nation-wide basis, with the average failure rate being less than 5 per cent.

Students who pass all their examinations and obtain the required credits are awarded diplomas which equal those of two- or three-year conventional colleges and institutions. The status of the RTVU graduates is guaranteed by government documentation which promises the same payment and future promotion for their qualifications as other students. In 1990 a quality and cost-effectiveness survey showed that more than 80 per cent of RTVU graduates were considered fully qualified by their employers.

Course development

China's Radio and TV universities provide courses in three categories: core courses, continuing education courses, and courses produced on the basis of local needs. The first two categories are mainly prepared by the Central Radio and TV University in Beijing. These are courses for which there is a consistent nation-wide interest and need. The third category is usually produced by the provincial radio and television universities based on the needs assessment of local social and economic development.

The course development procedure is that approval for distance education development is first given by the State Education Commission or by the local education authorities. Courses are then developed by course teams composed of the RTVU lecturers, media personnel and academics from conventional universities. The whole course development process takes from three to five years, depending on the curriculum and expertise of the team. The RTVU courses are multi-media, consisting of radio and television broadcasting, audio and video recordings, as well as printed materials.

Student support services

Student support service is provided in the form of compulsory group tuition in China's Radio and TV universities. This service is offered through thousands of RTVU study centres established in local RTVUs and the work covers the provision of classrooms, facilities and equipment, face-to-face tutorials, guidance and counselling, as well as the administration of student affairs.

Essential to understanding the system is the realization that many of the students receive three years' study leave on full pay. The application for enrolment in distance education in many cases is initiated by the company and if approved by the company manager the employee has by law no work for three to five years, depending on the study programme.

The student, therefore, attends at work during the study period but goes to the company Education Centre and not to the factory. The study programme usually lasts from 8.30 to 12.00 and from 1.30 to 4.30 and consists of three TV lectures per day by satellite from the CRTVU in Beijing, plus face-to-face lectures in the company's education centre in groups of twenty, during which the tutors go through the textbooks, students do assignments and the tutor gives evaluation and feedback. The students have to attend.

Costs

The budget for the network comes from a variety of sources. The Central Radio and TV University is funded by the State Education Commission, with China Central Television and China Educational Television being responsible for transmission costs and the Ministry of Posts and Telecommunications being responsible for the recurrent fees paid to hundreds of microwave relay stations and satellite communication services (Wei and Tong 1994).

Regional TVUs at provincial and regional levels get their financial support from provincial and regional governments with the education centres and tutorial groups being funded by educational bureaux of local governments, industries and public services.

An estimated 59 per cent of the total budget comes from official sources. Of this only 7.4 per cent (4.4 per cent of the total) comes from Central Government with 92.6 per cent (54.6 per cent of the total) coming from local governments at different levels. Students pay 4.3 per cent of the total, and the rest (36.7 per cent) of the total is paid in tuition fees by the employers of the students.

GROUP 3: THE DEPARTMENT OF INDEPENDENT STUDY AND DISTANCE EDUCATION OF THE UNIVERSITY OF FLORIDA AT GAINESVILLE

Institution

The Department of Independent Study and Distance Education is a section of the Division of Continuing Education of the University of Florida. Address: 1221 NW 13th Street, Gainesville, Florida, 32609. USA. Telephone: 001904–3921701.

Structure

The University of Florida is one of the ten public universities which comprise Florida's state university system.

One of the many administrative structures within the University of Florida is the Division of Continuing Education. The purpose of the Division of Continuing Education is to contribute to a learning society by helping students pursue educational interests at home, on campus and in the community, while they are actively working or meeting personal and family objectives.

The Department of Independent Study and Distance Education is one of the departments of the Division of Continuing Education. This department has been designated in state law as the only distance education programme to serve all the public universities in the Florida system.

Staffing

The director of the Department of Independent Study has a full-time staff of twenty who run a single centralized office through which all registrations and assignments flow. In 1994 the Department utilized 112 faculty who were employed in the academic departments of several of Florida's public universities; no faculty members are employed full-time in distance education.

The Vice-President for Academic Affairs of the university supervises all academic areas, and the deans of the respective colleges under him supervise the conventional staff. The Dean of Continuing Education reports to the Vice-President for Academic Affairs, so in an organizational sense continuing education is parallel to but separately organized from the faculties in the colleges of the university.

Conventional staff are utilized as part-time faculty of the Division of Continuing Education for all university credit courses at a distance and on campus, teaching in an overload status for which they draw additional compensation. High school teachers from the university's Laboratory School, also on the regular faculty, teach most of the high school courses offered at a distance by the university.

Students and courses

The total enrolment in the department in the 1993/4 academic year was 4,965. Of these 49 per cent were in undergraduate university courses, 11 per cent in high school programmes and 40 per cent in non-credit courses. With 4,965 enrolments the University of Florida was one of the largest of the eighty United States universities affiliated to the Independent Study Division of the National University Continuing Education Association.

Typical student groups were: full-time students who, due to courses being unavailable on-campus or job conflicts, take external courses as an alternative; adults working on external degrees elsewhere; and high school students who must make up missed or failed courses. There are limitations imposed by most of the faculties of United States universities on the use of independent study credits towards degree programmes and in many cases one is not permitted to complete a full degree at a distance. This is particularly so at Master's level.

Success and quantity of provision

There is usually a less than 2 per cent failure in courses done by independent study, though some who are doing poor work may elect not to complete their courses and thus avoid a failing grade. In 1993/4 there were 4,965 registrations and 2,728 completions; 210 students formally dropped their enrolments, usually receiving a partial refund of the fee paid. Another 453 students extended their expiring enrolment through the payment of an additional fee.

Since 55 per cent of students completed their courses, there was a 45 per cent non-completion rate for the year. There is not adequate data to distinguish those who have permanently dropped out from those who have temporarily discontinued their studies.

Quality of provision and status

Each university course study guide is prepared by a regular member of the faculty and the content of the course is based on the course taught for the academic department on-campus.

Once the course study guide has been edited, illustrated and published, the content is co-ordinated with and approved by the academic department chairperson before the course is opened to student enrolment. Students are required to obtain a counsellor's permission to enrol if they plan to apply the credit earned at a distance to meet degree requirements. Thus, to the extent possible, the independent study programme is integrated with the conventional system.

The university courses fall under the accreditation system of the Southern Association of Colleges and Schools, one of the regional accrediting associations that accredit all university education in the United States. Individual courses that may be applied to degrees are offered, but not an external degree.

Non-credit courses do not require accreditation, but each is co-ordinated and approved by the state agency or professional association that establishes continuing professional education requirements in its field.

Course development

Each course is prepared by the faculty member who is to teach it. Course production staff provide support in the form of editing, word processing, obtaining needed copyright permission, artwork, and desktop publishing. Most courses have illustrations and diagrams printed in the study guides. Also used are audiotapes (both commercial and locally prepared), videotapes (prepared by the university's College of Engineering), cloth samples, rock kits, seed kits and sets of 35 mm slides. Sixty of the courses are available on email.

In all courses the course evaluation standards of the National University Continuing Education Association are rigorously applied. This has resulted in national awards for course excellence.

Student support services

Student support services include toll-free phone lines serving students anywhere in the US, State University System libraries that provide books, periodicals, and photocopies of articles. Numerous instructors regularly meet in their offices or by telephone or by email with independent study students on an appointment basis.

The range of college courses, continuing professional education non-credit courses, and high school courses that have been put on email allows students to send in assignments at any time and from anywhere in the world and receive back their graded assignments by email.

Costs

The total cost per year (1994) of the distance education system was over $1.2 million. This includes salaries, expenses, instructor grading and other part-time services. The sources of funds for the 1993/4 academic year were: state government 32 per cent, non-credit course fees 38 per cent, book store operations 23 per cent, and reserves 7 per cent.

The non-credit course fees combine high school and non-credit fees paid by students; these programmes are required to be self-supporting. The book store is also required to be self-supporting. Income from state government is intended to offset the cost of operating the university credit programme. Fees collected from students for registration in university courses are returned to the state government which, in turn, gives an allocation per year based on need.

GROUP 4: CONTACT NORTH/CONTACT NORD, THUNDER BAY AND SUDBURY, ONTARIO, CANADA

Institution

Contact North/Contact Nord is a programme of the Government of Ontario. It has a North West Regional Co-ordinating Centre at Thunder Bay which works mainly in English. Telephone: 001807–3463101. It has a North East Regional Co-ordinating Centre at Sudbury which works in both English and French. Telephone 001705–6712710.

Structure

Contact North/Contact Nord is a programme of the Government of Ontario. The main members of the consortium that implement it are the North West Regional Centre at Thunder

203

Bay, the North East Regional Centre at Sudbury, Confederation College at Thunder Bay, Lakehead University at Thunder Bay, Cambrian College at Sudbury and Laurentian University at Sudbury. The basic structure is that the courses are provided by the colleges and universities (and a number of schools) and the two regional co-ordinating centres do not provide courses but provide student support services and partnership arrangements with 196 remote communities (many of which have no road access) to allow residents to take courses that would otherwise not be available to them.

Staffing

Contact North employs 179 site co-ordinators in remote communities, 19 full-time, 160 part-time. The 22 full-time and 13 part-time staff employed at the NE and NW Regional Co-ordinating Centres are mainly community liaison and telecommunications networking specialists. Those at Sudbury are bilingual in French and English, those at Thunder Bay mainly English-speaking. Each of the four contracting colleges/universities has a Distance Education Centre with part-time or full-time staff.

Students and courses

In the September 1994 to June 1995 academic year 396 courses were offered in English: 43 at secondary level, 267 at college level and 86 at university level to a student enrolment of 8,232. In French there were 11 secondary level courses, 26 college courses and 25 university courses for an enrolment of 650.

Success and quantity of provision

The number of students registered to take courses over the network approached 10,000 in 1995. In recent years there has been a steady increase in university-level and college-level enrolments and a considerable increase in secondary level. In 1995 8 per cent of the enrolment was at secondary level, 62 per cent at college level and 30 per cent at university level.

Quality of provision and status

Contact North provides the electronic network for provincially funded education institutions to deliver courses to residents of Northern Ontario. The achievement is for courses from the institutions to be delivered to remote communities of the same quality as at the institutions themselves by means of the electronic networks and on-side co-ordinators provided by the two regional co-ordinating centres at Thunder Bay and Sudbury.

Course development

Within the consortium, the two co-ordinating centres do not have any courses nor do they control what is delivered. This is the role of the universities, the colleges and the secondary providers. The courses are developed by the universities, colleges and secondary providers and arranged for distance education use by their Distance Education Centres.

Student support services

Once the students have enrolled and the courses are developed it is the role of the two regional co-ordinating centres to achieve the linkages to the remote communities. The main technologies used are audioconferencing and audiographics (audioconferencing with electronic blackboard and slides) and, in some courses, compressed videoconferencing. These networks are owned and controlled by Contact North, and the contracting institutions book time on them.

Costs

The aim is to provide courses to students in remote communities in Northern Ontario at no additional cost at the remote site. The cost to the student should be the same as if the course was taken at Thunder Bay or Sudbury. Contact North pays the costs of all electronic communication links and the costs of site operation.

EVALUATION

GROUP 5: THE DISTANCE EDUCATION CENTRE OF THE UNIVERSITY OF NEW ENGLAND, AUSTRALIA

Institution

The University of New England is at Armidale, New South Wales, Australia 2351. Telephone: 006167–733333.

Structure

The University of New England's Vice-Chancellor is the chief executive and reports of the University Council chaired by the Chancellor. There are, in 1995, two Deputy Vice-Chancellors, one responsible for academic matters, the other for resources and planning and a half-time Pro Vice-Chancellor Research. The Distance Education Centre (DEC) comes within the purview of the Deputy Vice-Chancellor Academic. The DEC consists of two units, the Distance and Open Learning Unit and the Materials Development Unit.

Staffing

The Distance Education Centre has a full-time administrative staff of slightly less than forty and is headed by a director. DEC staff are responsible for instructional design/course development, the production and distribution of unit materials (in excess of 750), processing the receipt and return of assignments and administrative matters associated with the organization of residential schools.

Some 500 full-time academics are involved in delivering distance education units. Part-time staff are employed on a restricted basis.

Students and courses

The enrolment of the university in 1995 was 14,800: 10,300 studying externally, the remaining 4,500 being internal.

When the university was inaugurated in 1955 it taught both internally and externally. The external provision was originally to meet the needs of a shortage of graduate teachers in New South Wales. In 1964 82 per cent of the external enrolments were

206

teachers and numbered 2,263; by 1983 the proportion of teachers had fallen to 28 per cent.

Today the University of New England gives external access to associate diplomas, bachelor degrees, graduate certificates, graduate diplomas, masters and Ph.D. degrees for 108 separate awards (eighty-five at postgraduate level) in a wide range of disciplines.

Of the external students 70 per cent are studying for undergraduate degrees; the remaining 30 per cent for postgraduate qualifications.

The student population is heterogeneous. In 1994 63 per cent were female, ages were from 20 to 80, and students had varied educational and work backgrounds. Students enrol externally because of isolation from tertiary institutions, because of family commitments, work commitments, or a preference for individual study.

Success and quantity of provision

In any one year 82–5 per cent of distance students who submit for final assessment are successful. In terms of university merit lists and awards, external students figure prominently.

Drop-out is highest among new students. Since 1983 there has been a noticeable downward trend in withdrawal rates from 26.9 per cent in 1983 to 4.7 per cent in 1994. As there is no time limit on first degree completion, students 'drop-in' and drop-out' of the external system as their circumstances dictate.

Quality of provision and status

The status of learning at a distance and of awards is accepted as being of the same standard as the conventional part of the university. The degrees and awards are the same for distance students as for the on-campus students and are accredited by the university.

The external courses provide a university education; there is a minor element of training in a limited number of programmes. The quality of the external programme is underpinned by the following provisions:

- compulsory residential schools for the majority of units;
- the obligation on distance students to see their university and enjoy a brief period of traditional university life as a full-time student in residence;
- optional weekend seminars;
- distance students being brought into contact with the best brains of the university, not part-time staff.

Course development

Courses are designed by individual academics usually with support from specialist development staff.

Print is the medium used in most courses and is supported by audio (large proportion of courses), audio-vision (fairly common), video and videoconferencing (small proportion). The use of interactive radio and TV is well developed.

Student support services

Day-to-day student support, including enrolment, is provided by each of the four Faculty Offices. Some assistance is provided by individual on-campus academics. Distance Education Centre staff provide specialist support.

Heavy reliance is placed on the telephone, mail, email and fax. Residential schools are compulsory in approximately 70 per cent of all external courses. These are held mainly in Armidale in the New South Wales country about 500 km north-west of Sydney. Voluntary weekend schools are usually conducted in Sydney, some in other centres in New South Wales and in Brisbane.

Support is also provided in a decentralized way through graduate representatives, regional advisers, and a Sydney Centre which operates in conjunction with three other rural New South Wales universities.

Costs

The total cost of the distance system was in the order of $30 million (Australian) in 1994. The source of funds was almost entirely from the recurrent grant of the Federal Australian Government.

208

REFERENCES

Keegan, D. and Rumble, G. (1982) 'The DTUs: an appraisal', pp. 222–50 in G. Rumble and K. Harry (eds) *The Distance Teaching Universities*, London: Croom Helm.

Wei, R. and Tong, Y. (1994) *Radio and TV Universities: The Mainstream of China's Adult and Distance Higher Education*, Nanjing: Yilin Press.

12

CONCLUSION

That's what I'm trying to do. Sing a better song.
Educating Rita, 1983

Distance education is a little-studied area of education which is growing in importance annually. As a more industrialized form of educational provision it is well adapted to the developments of new communications technologies and brings to education many of the strengths and dangers of industrialization. It is also adapted to the growth of privacy in post-industrial societies which focuses many of the functions of living on the individual's residence with a concomitant loss of the sense of community in society.

The conclusions from the study are many and varied but are not put forward here as judgements which are to be considered normative for practice. Rather they are put forward as suggestions for research by scholars and invitations to others to contribute to our knowledge of the theory and practice of distance education.

Among the most important are:

- distance education is a coherent and distinct field of educational endeavour;
- distance education is a distinct field of education, parallel to and a complement of conventional education. It has its own didactic laws, administrative procedures and characteristic buildings and plant;
- distance education is a needed component of many national education systems;
- the correct term for this sector of education is 'distance education';

- it is possible to propose a coherent definition of distance education which distinguishes it from other areas of educational activity;

- distance education institutions can be classified into five major groupings;

- distance systems can be cheaper but this depends on a complex range of factors, some of which may affect the quality of provision;

- distance systems have inherent difficulties with the quantity, quality, and status of provision;

- cohesive and competently administered systems can solve the problems of quantity, quality, and status of provision (examples are given of institutions which appear to have achieved acceptable solutions); and

- distance education is a legitimate field of academic enquiry.

The study accepts Pagney's (1980) position that distance education is complementary to conventional provision. Distance education is the normal provision of education for the working man and woman, for the taxpayer, the home-maker, those who do not wish to attend a conventional institution, and sometimes for their children. Conventional education is the normal provision for others.

No government can provide schools, colleges, and universities near the workplace of every citizen and few can provide for citizens outside the 5–25 years age bracket. Distance education is a needed component of most national education systems.

As the 1980s progressed towards the 1990s the loss of community involvement in many western societies and the consequent growth of privatization of living were seen by some as further indications of the permanency of education at a distance (Smith 1987).

The challenge taken up by distance educators is to provide at a distance an educational experience that achieves parity with conventional provision in quality, quantity and status.

CURRENT ISSUES

The rationale for distance education does not lie in the notion that there is something wrong with conventional education that distance education should correct. This is a dangerous cul-de-sac. The reply can be withering:

A few years ago 'non-traditional learning' was touted as a mechanism to democratise education. Today ministers of education are happily hacking at 'traditional' institutions which are easily replaced by 'distance education'. There is a vast irony in all this because distance education was supposed to help democratise educational processes; few anticipated it would be a weapon used to beat the heads of institutions where learners and teachers have the temerity to gather together to learn in groups.

(Boshier 1985: 139)

It is distressing to find that distance educators continue their criticism of conventional schooling and university lecturing as the twentieth century draws to its close. This criticism of on-campus programmes calls for the improvement of on-campus education, not for the development or funding of distance systems.

Many of the contemporary evaluations of distance education and its role in future educational provision are quite favourable. Portway and Lane give this assessment from an American source:

Distance education is more than just another attempt by the education community to respond to the rising chorus of criticism leveled at it by citizens, school boards and government. It is a discernible step in social education. It is an imaginative and yet practical attempt by society to invest itself with the survival skills needed in a highly competitive world that increasingly values the educated, cooperative, technologically competent citizen. Distance education provides a sorely needed fresh perspective. It forces our thinking beyond the confines of the campus and out into the changing world.

(Portway and Lane 1994: 168)

In spite of such upbeat analyses there are, nevertheless, a range of issues which contribute to the frailty of the foundations of distance education: lack of professionalization of the field; failure to contribute to general education theory; confusion about whether distance education is to be regarded as a form of education or a didactic mode; lack of grounded theory on the educational effectiveness and the cost-effectiveness of various technologies.

The development in the 1990s of bachelors, masters and doctoral degrees in distance education has not yet led to a professionalization of the field. In spite of some excellent preliminary work (Parer 1995) and a growing focus on quality control, both of materials development and student support services, there is little agreement yet on what constitutes competence in distance education or lack of competence. The consequence is that there are as yet no guidelines on how employment in the field is to be organized.

In this book distance education is seen as a distinct field of educational research with its own small, but unique, contribution to make to general education theory and practice. It has specific contributions to make in areas where conventional schools, colleges and universities have difficulties coping with citizens' needs: the design and logistics of very large education systems capable of handling competently over 100,000 students at a time; solutions to the problem of streaming (a major feature when students are grouped for instruction); the education of prisoners, the disabled (Ommerborn 1994), the disadvantaged, those who will not travel to the schools, colleges and universities that society builds for the provision of education.

This study takes the position (with Peters 1973, 1996) that distance education is a form of educational provision and that it can provide a complete educational offering from counselling and enrolment to certification and graduation, often many years later. It is a field for educational research, a suitable subject for the awarding of university degrees and a complex form of educational provision with many didactic modes. There is the correspondence mode, the study-centre mode, the consultation mode, the Australian integrated mode, the one-way-video two-way-audio mode, the two-way-video two-way-audio mode, and many more. The significance of the field of research and the basis for offering university degrees in distance education are dissipated for those who describe the field as a mode of teaching.

In spite of the long association of the field with the use of technological media, there is as yet little grounded theory on the cost-effectiveness and the educational effectiveness of the use of media in distance systems. The classic studies of Dubin and Taveggia (1968), Schramm (1973) and Clark (1983) have shown clearly enough that one technological medium cannot be claimed to be didactically superior to any other medium. This means that one does not have to be rich to learn and that one does not have to enrol in a system with expensive technologies to study with success. Much of the success of this form of education in the developed, and certainly in the developing, world is due to economies of scope and economies of scale from reproducing a great number of cheaply produced, but didactically sound, materials.

CONCLUSION

As the twenty-first century arrives solidly grounded foundations of distance education are required for its role as a provider of education in the years to come. The perspective of this study is that educational provision at the end of the 1990s is enriched by the availability, for the first time in history, of conventional, distance and virtual systems. Conventional education, which developed well before the Industrial Revolution, continues to flourish in the schools, colleges and universities of the world today, providing education for hundreds of millions of students.

Born of the Industrial Revolution in the mid-nineteenth century, distance education finally achieved recognition nearly a generation ago after a difficult and sometimes chequered first one hundred years. It flourishes today in open universities, company training centres, distance training colleges and open, flexible and distance departments of conventional institutions providing education for tens of millions of students today.

The breathtaking array of communications technologies produced by the Electronics Revolution of the 1980s made their way into educational provision in the late 1980s, making it possible to teach face to face at a distance. Electronic classrooms hundreds or thousands of kilometres apart were linked by compressed video, satellite or full bandwidth linkages into a virtual system.

The provision of education today is enriched by having conventional, distance and virtual systems complementing each other and enriching provision for citizens. It is too early to decide whether virtual systems will be studied in the future as a subset of distance education or as a field of study in their own right.

At the beginning of the new millenium crucial decisions face international planners and government agencies on the investment of taxpayers' monies in the provision of education. Do they build and maintain buildings to which students will travel for face-to-face group-based conventional education, or do they choose to fund distance education or invest citizens' monies in the development of virtual educational provision?

REFERENCES

Boshier, R. (1985) Book review. *The International Review of Education* 31(1), 139–40.

Clark, R. (1983) 'Reconsidering research on learning from media', *Review of Educational Research* 53(4), 445–59.

Dubin, R. and Taveggia, T. (1968) *The Teaching–learning Paradox. A Comparative Analysis of College Teaching Methods*, Eugene: University of Oregon.

Ommerborn, R. (1994) *Fernstudium für Behinderte: Voraussetzungen, Formen und Möglichkeiten*, Engelsbach: Hänsel-Hohenhausen.

Pagney, B. (1980) 'Quels advantages l'enseignement à distance peut-il offrir à l'enseignement formel', EHSC Conference, April.

Parer, M. (1995) 'Good distance teaching: quality distance teaching = structured design + dialogue + communication', in D. Sewart (ed.) *One World Many Voices: Quality in Open and Distance Learning*, Milton Keynes: Open University.

Peters, O. (1973) *Die didaktische Struktur des Fernunterrichts*. Weinheim: Beltz.

Peters, O (1996) 'Distance education is a form of teaching and learning sui generis', *Open Learning* 1, 10–15.

Portway, P. and Lane, C. (eds) *(1994) Guide to Teleconferencing and Distance Learning*, San Ramon Calif.: Applied Business Telecommunications.

Schramm, W. (1973) *Big Media, Little Media*, London: Sage.

Smith, P. (1987) 'Distance education and educational change', in P. Smith and M. Kelly (eds) *Distance Education and the Mainstream*, London: Croom Helm.

INDEX